Charlie Bermant's *Never Enough* includes the up front recollections of changing times, during which time music, culture and technology evolved together. Told through shifting viewpoints, these stories reflect a desire to get closer and learn more about the music and the musicians. These stories provide a unique view of interesting times, in a voice that is often self-deprecating but never depressing.

For Rudy Hopkins

"If I don't meet you no more in this world then I'll meet you in the next one. Don't be late." -Jimi Hendrix

Transcript/1

———

OK, we are in the KWTK-FM studios, July 10, 2017. Reference Char   Bermant, "Never Enough," begin recording.

Thanks for coming in and sorry that you had to wait. The autobiographical poem our last guest was reading ran a little longer than expected.

Thank you for inviting me.

It seems like there are a lot of these books coming out now, recalling the 1960s in detail. Why do you think that is? And who cares?

Everyone thinks their era was special and the most defining time in modern history, but mine actually was. I have ridden two huge cultural waves. Social, with the 1960s creating a cultural thunderstorm that uprooted everything that happened before. And technological, where new stuff emerged so rapidly you barely recognize what the world was just a few years before.

The musical sweet spot for me was between 1965 and 1975. Some of it is crap, and I hear stuff I used to like and just cringe. My favorites, I've heard them a million times but they still make me smile or cry. And there are some things from that time that I missed the first time and am getting into now.

The tech stuff still changes and grows every few months and that can be pretty scary. When I was a kid my dad would take me around the car dealerships every fall to look at the new models. These days, phones get the same upgrade treatment. Do parents these days take their kids to wireless stores? I can't keep up anymore, but seeing the arrival of the first personal computers and the reactions of people to them was pretty cool.

But your book is mostly about music. You don't really talk much about tech except for that one chapter.

That's another book by someone else. I cover some stuff from the early '90s when everyone knew tech could do something for music but they weren't sure just what. Then the Internet came along and it became clear how to connect tech and music. Up till then no one knew what would work and what would crash. So it was a cool time, but really frustrating.

In such times it's always fun to be a journalist because you get stuff for free. But if you are a consumer and actually want to accomplish something or have to pay for it, you should probably wait.

I'm still a little puzzled. You seem to be a talented writer, but have spent most of your life writing about inconsequential things. And in the dawn of the most frightening and fractious period of modern history, you are selling us a book that does nothing to improve those conditions or make people aware of the important stuff. Aren't you a little ashamed and embarrassed about that?

Not really.

And the format here is a bit confusing. First you write about Woodstock, which is interesting, but then you try to tell your story through second-person narrative and journal entries. How much of this is real? Did you keep all of these from when you wrote them, or did you just fill in the blanks?

I was trying to break things up. To not tell the same stories the same way. To paint a big picture using little pieces. Read the whole thing and you know what it was like to be there, or at least what it was like to be me.

When I was sixteen, I had no intention of becoming a writer but sensed that writing provided a path to temporary sanity. If I could write these things down maybe I could read them over and see what made sense, and what didn't. I started filling up notebooks with brutally honest, barely legible long-hand scribblings. I still have them. Every few years I take them out of one box and put them in another. I have never read them, and not because they were indecipherable. As the words poured out I recognized their value, but that was the end of it. Although I might not have known that at the time.

Why don't you publish the original journals? Seems like they would be a bit more authentic.

In order to publish them I'd have to read and edit them. And I'm not going to read them. Too revealing. Too embarrassing. Too personal. Too illegible.

You didn't answer the other question. How much of these so-called journals are actually real?

They are not the original journals; they are recreated. I recall the time quite well so I just put myself back into those days and wrote what I remembered. Or I don't, and just write how it probably happened. It may not be exactly true but it's close enough for non-fiction.

But they aren't real.

So what? All recollections go through a filter. It can't be false, but it needs to be entertaining or at least interesting. As you pointed out, any random yahoo can write a book and you need to make it different enough to keep people interested.

I didn't say that at all. That's another example of you bending the truth to support whatever point that you are trying to prove.

This is my little project. If its boundaries offend you, don't read it. Or better yet, write something your own self.

Point taken. But I'm still not sure that you've given us a very good reason to read this book. Unlike your last book, which had a lot of interviews, this is mostly about you. And with all due respect, you're not any more exciting than other people who lived through this. Like myself.

Yeah, you're right, I have a harder sell on this book and it was more difficult to write. *A Serious Hobby*, which I published in 2012, was a collection of my celebrity interviews, slightly edited and connected by a theme, which was pretty much ego-driven. I began writing it as a way to brag, and it was only during the later drafts that I realized it was something other people might actually read. That turned out to be true, pretty much. I didn't sell many books but people light up when I give them a copy.

How many of them actually read it, all the way through?

Maybe none of them. I never ask. Not because it's intrusive, I really don't want to know.

How did the new book come about?

It actually began as an update of *A Serious Hobby*. I wanted to clean up some of the writing, edit the pictures and revise a few chapters. The one about Ian Hunter, specifically. I'd been a big fan of his since Mott The Hoople days, and this was the third time I'd attempted to interview him. I saw that particular piece as a way to come full circle in the book.

I had two misfires interviewing Hunter. In 1975 I had set it up to talk to him and guitarist Mick Ronson after the show at the Spectrum in Philadelphia. I liked the show well enough, but was pumped about the interview. So I didn't notice the flaws and miscues that upset the band. After spending what seemed like hours in the hall outside the dressing room they emerged, still barking at each other. When I asked about the interview the road manager patiently explained the obvious, that it wasn't going to happen.

In 1988, right after I moved to Portland, Hunter and Ronson were passing through town. Instead of the cavernous Spectrum they played in a small club off of Broadway. I set up the interview and met them in their dressing room, where it became obvious neither one was in a good mood. Hunter answered questions briefly and without enthusiasm, while Ronson spent the whole time lying on a ratty couch. Hunter only came to life when I told him that I was to be married in a few weeks, offering a litany of reasons why I should not take the plunge. I was having doubts, so I wondered "how did he know" before determining that I wasn't going to let some fading rock star deter me from my life's plan.

They weren't giving me anything I could use, and it only took a few minutes to wonder why I was there. It was so discouraging that I didn't even transcribe the tape.

Still, I was pumped to chat with Hunter, and was scheduled to meet him at his hotel prior to his Bumbershoot gig in 2012. An hour before I was set to go downtown I got a call from his PR guy who said that Hunter didn't want to do an in-person, and it needed to be on the phone. Which threw me. I wasn't set up to tape over the phone.

I ended up doing the interview in the car, talking to him on speaker and using my iPad to record. Except he couldn't hear half of what I was asking and misunderstood the other half.

I still wrote a positive article, but felt guilty about it. I was going to rewrite the chapter and tell people what I really felt, that I wasn't sure why I had pursued a Hunter interview for thirty years. It was a good thing that I had other stuff going on in the meantime. So I didn't feel like I wasted my life.

I did the rewrite but then decided to start a whole new book. But the Hunter chapter didn't make the cut because it was too snarky. Most of it was questioning why I spent so much time and energy on someone who wasn't all that interesting. Which itself was not that interesting.

I did carry over a few chapters from *A Serious Hobby*. The Garth Hudson story fit right in. As did the "Wheelchair Legends" narrative. I also expounded on the George Harrison piece. I didn't feel enough people read the first book, so readers won't feel cheated.

You've done a lot of stupid things for music. And wasted a lot of your life.

Not a waste. Not at all. There are things I would have done differently, of course, but in general it's been a pretty good ride. I've had a lot of fun getting close to the music.

Admittedly I made some dumb decisions. A lot of times, I'd look forward so fiercely to an event or concert or interview that I missed the event itself. It was over as if it never happened and I didn't even have any clear memories. To scale it down to a more practical level it was similar to traveling four hours each way for a ninety-minute show.

Which I did more than a few times between DC, New York, Boston, Providence and Philadelphia, in various combinations. We'd get tickets for a show several hours away and drive all of the day and all of the night to get there. Philadelphia for Bowie and the Spiders, to the Bronx to cheer for The Kinks. We'd spend three times longer driving than watching the show but that didn't really matter. We were spending nights on the road driving from one city to the next. But it was the rest of the world, those living regular lives, were the crazy ones.

So yeah, I did lots of stupid things for music but I wasn't an idiot, necessarily.

The chapter on Diana Rigg says a lot about her but maybe more about you. Weren't you something of a stalker here? Some of it is kind of creepy and would land you in jail today.

I didn't think I was doing anything weird or creepy. A week after interviewing her in DC I snuck through the backstage door in New York and surprised her. She was wearing what looked like a bathing cap. I guess that she tucked her own hair under the cap and put the wig over it. Her reaction made it clear that I shouldn't be there right then. She had already given me thirty minutes of her time and that was all I was going to get.

Up to that point I was trying to write something really good that showed my appreciation of her. I wanted her to read it and like me. I didn't want to be her friend. I wouldn't be able to handle the pressure. I wanted her to like me, but that one sharp look made it clear that was never going to happen.

It took a few years before I figured out that the people I interviewed never liked me. I shouldn't have expected anything different. Talking to me was part of their job. They are nice to me for the duration of the interview. When I walked out of a room or hung up the phone I was out of their lives, forever. That didn't stop me right away because I thought I could add some value.

Diana Rigg and Jerry Lewis seem out of place in a book about rock 'n' roll.

Not really. Diana Rigg was part of that 1960s British infatuation. It started with the music but we wanted more, so films and TV shows about England filled the bill. Jerry Lewis is not rock 'n' roll, but I included it because it was about celebrity, and my ability to observe a situation rather than attempt to participate. But I guess the real answer is that this is my book and these are my stories. It doesn't have to fit in a neat little box.

You did meet some other big-deal people. How did you pull that off?

I'd find a target, then sell the idea of an interview to a publication. I would figure out the places where the performer would appear and contact papers in that market. This worked only for a little while, until everyone else caught on. When papers went online people in one town could easily read a newspaper from another so I couldn't sell to individual markets. When blogging caught on and everyone became their own publisher it got even worse. Using journalism to meet your heroes became a transparent ruse. Some of the musicians believed the flattery, while it became harder to get to the ones who still had some relevance. The good news is that my idea of relevance didn't usually match everyone else's.

You sound bitter, and that's not really an attractive... Hold on a sec, we have to cut this short (buzzing) hello? Since when? Shit. Charlie, we are going to need to do this again. The recording chip was damaged. And we have someone else coming in now. Can you come in, say in two or three weeks, so we can recut? And maybe you can be a little more specific about why people should read this.

Seriously? You book me a month ahead of time, you're late getting started, kick me out early, and then want me to come back and do it over? Doesn't really show a lot of respect. Not that I'm a celebrity or anything.

You do know that technology isn't perfect, and this happens all the time.

Really? I thought you had these great backup systems. And if the chip was damaged and there's no recording, where did this transcript come from?

Fuck you, man.

Takeoff

———

Small children believe they are the only people in the world, then accommodate others as they grow. Teenagers go through their own behavior portal. While they are at the center of their own universe, the air seems thicker than the bracketing epochs of childhood and adulthood.

Everyone needs to grow up somewhere, with that place taking on special qualities for the rest of their lives. History marches on, with a differing experience for those who live where they occur. In the 1960s and 1970s those who grew up in historical flashpoints such as Woodstock, New York and Washington DC earned special qualities. In that sense, the belief that I was at the center of the universe was true.

Everyone remembers their fourth grade year as special. Mine really was. John F. Kennedy was shot in the fall, and the Beatles arrived in the spring. They were on the *Ed Sullivan Show* on three consecutive Sundays. For the first two we were sitting in Poughkeepsie surrounded by boxes, on the third we were unpacking those same boxes in our new home at the end of a Woodstock cul-de-sac.

In Woodstock there was a feeling that something was happening there and you almost knew what it was, even if you were only eleven. Bob Dylan lived there, or so we were told.

Our paths crossed once. My parents took us to *The Marriage of Figaro* in a small theater in the middle of the woods. Before the show I saw the back of a frizzy head and said aloud "Hey, that's Bob Dylan," just to fill the silence. Dad didn't seem to hear. He said, "Hey, that's Joe Resnick," pointing to a round

9

guy in a suit sitting up front. I knew that name. He was our new congressman for whom I'd campaigned for the previous year, standing atop a wooden wire stool to a crowd of juvenile non-voters.

At intermission Resnick was nice enough, but he asked dumb questions and treated me like a kid. Which I was. By the time I looked for Dylan, intermission was over. When the lights came up after the show he was gone.

Peter Yarrow, of Peter, Paul and Mary, was in the Woodstock phone book. But no one in our little group had the stones to call him up and invite him to our little peace march on the Village Green. As for Dylan, we all knew he lived up the mountain and had been injured in a motorcycle wreck. Some kids at school claimed to have seen the wreck but offered no proof.

Mike Mondore (left) and Charlie playing a co-ed party in 1967. This was taken minutes before a humiliating game of "Spin the Bottle" and the composition of "Everybody Hates Me." Which Charlie and Mike rehearsed but never could get right.

At the end of the summer, my parents took us to Greenwich Village for an afternoon. I knew New York and had seen the big white arch a few times, but this trip downtown was magic.

I ditched my parents, sort of. I was always ten steps ahead so no one would know that I was on a leash. The place was jammed with button stores and record shops.

I couldn't afford any records but landed a few buttons. One looked like it was in Hebrew but actually said GO FUCK YOUR SELF. Dad looked over my shoulder as I plunked down fifty cents for the button. I was caught. But he laughed and said that I shouldn't show it to my grandmother.

On McDougal Street we discovered Cafe Wha?, a basement down the stairs. They had a house band called The Raves. I hadn't seen any haircuts like theirs in real life before. They were shoulder-length on the sides with a little flip at the bottom, and bangs. Once they started playing we couldn't hear each other or speak so we just listened, drinking soda. After the band a hypnotist came onstage and asked for volunteers. I started to raise my hand but Mom stopped me.

The band came back and I got sucked into a particularly catchy song.
"Mr. Maaaaaan, uh huh.
Mr. Maaaaaan, uh huh."

The parents said it was time to leave. I wanted to stay a little longer. But I was an imposter on a strange planet so I decided I'd better not call attention to myself. Because I swore to return.

A few weeks later Dad called us to the living room and said we were moving. I immediately pictured living in Greenwich Village, but soon learned that the actual destination was Maryland. just outside of DC.

I was looking forward to the change. I knew I was cool. I knew things. I'd lived in Woodstock, so the Maryland kids would all gather around to hear stories about Bob Dylan and the Village Green. But I hedged my bets. On my last day of school in Woodstock I visited Mr. Hopkins, an English teacher who had mentioned that he was starting a camp and invited me to consider participating next summer. It was going to be small and artistic.

Probably not, I thought, I liked the idea of a larger camp. More girls, for one thing.

I got to the new school early and brimming with optimism. This lasted about three hours. I was pushed into was a fast environment where I was ignored by ninety percent of the kids and drew physical fire from the remainder.

Even with short hair and horn rims I appeared to have a giant neon BEATLES FAN sign above my head, and all the kids in my school liked Motown and Stax. Which to them meant they needed to dress in black leather and whack around anyone who didn't wear "soul" on their forehead. Considering the music's roots it was a little odd how the black kids didn't participate in any of the torture. They weren't going to participate in the bullying but they weren't going to make it any better for me, either.

Every day I'd walk over to the local shopping center and spend hours in the record store. I'd wade through the bins, where new records with bright covers by artists with extraterrestrial names would appear daily. Since there were so many I didn't know where to take a chance, but I learned their names before I heard a snippet of their music. The New York Rock and Roll Ensemble. The Peanut Butter Conspiracy. Orpheus. Chrysalis.

I bought Jimi Hendrix's *Axis:Bold as Love* and brought it to school to show how cool I was. I carried it around for a few days hoping that someone would see it and start a conversation. In music class the teacher asked if I wanted to play it for everybody, I said no. If these people didn't get the Beatles, there was no way they'd get Hendrix. Regular whacks on my head were going to happen anyway, but there was no reason to do something that would make it worse.

I spent winter break inside listening to records with titles like *Their Satanic Majesties' Request* and *After Bathing at Baxter's*. My record player was a small machine about four inches by ten inches that turned the records with a rubber wheel that made direct contact with the grooves. Which embedded gritty black rubber on the next to last track on each side.

Listening, and reading. Books sometimes, but mostly magazines and newspapers. We'd gone to New York twice over the holidays, each time I was able to buy a copy of *Beatles Monthly,* a British picture book the size of *TV Guide* that spoke for the group.

I had a few issues of *Crawdaddy,* which didn't look like other magazines. The type quality was one step above what we got off of the school mimeograph machine, but on better paper.

It felt like the *Crawdaddy* writers were talking to me directly, although on a slightly higher level than the average music magazine. There was a detailed review of *Sgt. Pepper,* and a detailed discussion of The Beach Boys, of all people.

Then a comparison of the Doors and the Kinks. I didn't really like either but still read the article many times. Along with the rest of the magazine, even the random notes section. Before too long I was sending letters to people in the same voice: *We've formed a band, and have added lead guitar, bass and drums.* In truth there was still only two of us and the band was mostly in our heads.

After a while I stopped guessing at how to befriend the bullies or even to decrease their ire. I give up, you win, just leave me alone. They didn't cooperate so I wrote Mr. Hopkins a letter, asking him to send me information about his camp.

When the brochure arrived I read it over and over, like it was an issue of *Crawdaddy!* This is what I wanted to do this summer, I told my parents. Me too, said my sister. Mom called Mr. Hopkins. It was settled: we would go there for the month of July.

In July the entire family drove from DC to the camp, in the middle of nowhere on the other side of the reservoir on a road I had never seen before. Mr. Hopkins was pushing a lawmower around. He greeted us and I introduced him to my parents. "Call me Rudy," he said. And we did, from then on.

The camp was a dilapidated set of buildings that Rudy's grandmother had run as a resort. Two long buildings were designated as boys' and girls' dorms. There was a lot of room because there were only four campers, two of each.

There was my four-years-younger sister Julie. There was Debbie, who smelled good and had a nice set of starter breasts that she would not let me see or touch, and Tim, an awkward kid from Pittsburgh.

Some camps had a bus. We got around in a whale of an Oldsmobile with four-on-the-floor and a 425-horsepower engine. The four campers were in the back seat, a tight fit for a two-door vehicle. Rudy and his wife, Dwight, would ride up front along with two-year-old Sean. I'd never met a two-year-old, or really paid attention to one.

I was so pumped to be in Woodstock, less than a year after we left. Mom suggested that I was expecting too much about going back, that if it weren't as I remembered it would come as a disappointment. That didn't happen. It wasn't a camp, but a family.

We did everything; swim, hike, go to movies, plays and concerts. The plays were all at the Woodstock Playhouse, a three-hundred-seat summer-stock venue where my family went at least twice a year when we lived there. This year they had concerts, from people I'd actually heard of. Mother Earth had a record out, so they were automatically cool. I'd heard them on the radio in DC and the lady, Tracy Nelson, who spent a lot of time apprenticing with people like Muddy Waters and Howlin' Wolf, had a nice voice.

I knew this, because I read *Crawdaddy!* and listened to the DJs who would always tell you something about each song they played. I knew a lot about musicians that I liked, and sometimes more about the ones I did not. I often hid this obscure knowledge from the people I would meet as it was embarrassing to let on that I knew these little details.

Also playing was Dave Van Ronk, who at that time was just another guy who made a few albums, and who my cousin Paul said was great. I would listen to these singers, disposed to like and understand what they were talking and singing about. Van Ronk didn't seem to have much to say. He sat on a stool in the middle of the stage, playing songs that I didn't know or particularly like. Except one, "Urge For Going," Joni Michell's tale of sadness and endings that I had learned to play myself. Van Ronk played the song with less emotion and skill than Tom Rush, like he was falling asleep. If someone really dug Dave Van Ronk they probably would have dug the show, but he left me cold.

When camp was halfway done we went to a Sound-Out, a lineup of bands in a meadow near Saugerties. I was anxious to see Chrysalis, not because of their music but because they had an album out and they were cool. I had never heard their music but had stared at their album during my daily visits to the record store in Bethesda.

I recognized the musicians, especially a blond guy with a mustache who played bass. I went up to him and struck up a conversation but he treated me like an awkward kid who wasn't worth his attention. Which I was.

Rudy was only eleven years older and soon became the anti-parent, as he supported rather than attempted to prevent outrageous or irresponsible behavior. In the same way, he pushed me when I got lazy and seemed to think that people should spend every waking moment actually doing something. He also made it clear when I said or did something really dumb.

"What's the name of your band?" he asked me when I told him of my planned little combo.

"Pieces," I said, showing him the logo I sketched out.

"That's a terrible name," he said. "The whole scene is all about moving together. Call yourself Pieces and you'll go against that."

Back home, I ended the summer with a Doors concert. Some kids had to drag their parents to shows as a condition of going. But three sets of parents decided that we were reliable enough to be dropped off and return to the same location three hours later.

Opening up, they slipped into its groove as lead singer Jim Morrison shouted out.

"I am ... I'm the back door man."

The first song, or even the first note, from an artist on a particular stage sets the mood for the evening and its memory. Some concerts start soft and get louder, but the best ones come out swinging. From that point that was my preference, a punch in the stomach rather than a stroke on the leg.

"Five to One," "Break on Through" and "When the Music's Over." It was moving so quickly that I couldn't catch up. I was knocked breathless by the fact I was really there, watching The Doors, that it was impossible to listen to the music. Although I heard it well enough.

Next was "Crystal Ship." I was finally in their sphere. Morrison sang the first three notes without the band: "Be ... fore ... you...."

The band came in on the fourth note but in a completely different key.

"...Slip...." Morrison's voice went up and the band descended. No one seemed to notice. After "Light My Fire," they left the stage. I couldn't believe it was over.

And it wasn't. They came back and Morrison spoke to us, asking what we wanted to hear next: "The End," which was eleven minutes of mystic noise; or the latest single, "The Unknown Soldier."

"The End" prevailed, although I yelled otherwise. Those who favored "The End" were thinking only of quantity. If it's a longer song we get more, and we want as much as we can get. I could go either way. But the songs up to now were the obvious ones, and I wanted to hear something different.

Morrison didn't act like he wanted to leave. I was sure that if he played "The Unknown Soldier" he would have extended it well beyond the three-minute radio version. "The End" didn't have a lot of variety and tended to meander for a while. It crashed to a close and actually seemed shorter than the record. I thought Morrison might have been punishing us. If we had yelled for "Unknown Soldier" and trusted him to expand it to a new place it would have been special. Instead it was ordinary, which was still pretty great.

Mike, Wayne and I started walking back to the rendezvous point where Mike's mother was going to pick us up, taking the long way around the amphitheater. People were walking behind us and were talking about what songs were left out.

"They didn't play 'People Are Strange,'" one said.

"I would have liked to hear that one," I said.

"Or 'Hello I Love You,'" another said.

Their latest single was a rip of the Kinks' "All the Day and All of the Night" from four years ago.

"I'm not content to...." I sang,

"... Be with you in the daytime,' Mike and Wayne started up.

"Girl I want to be with you all of the time. The only way I feel alright is by your side. Girl I want to be with you all of the time. All day and all of the night."

Those behind us didn't share our glee. I looked back and they were gone.

"They did play 'Five to One,'" Wayne said,

"I would like to see that again," I said. "I would like to see the whole thing again."

The following year was different. I had run away to New York City, lost my virginity and let my hair grow. No haircuts since September. I was looking forward to summer, especially when Rudy wrote me in March, telling me about "the biggest Sound-Out ever planned," in mid-August. Everyone who was anyone was going to be there, he said. Jefferson Airplane. Jimi Hendrix. Bob Dylan. No Beatles yet, but you could only hope.

We did the usual camp stuff which involved, oddly enough, camping. We swam, hiked and shopped. We went to plays and concerts at the Playhouse. We were only biding time until the big event. Tim Hardin was scheduled to play the festival, and did a show at the Playhouse a few weeks previously. I had heard one of his albums in April and it was stunning. I was already imagining the big festival where a red balloon soared above the crowd and he sang "Red Balloon."

The real Tim Hardin was gruff and raw and didn't quite reach all of the notes. It was live and I was seeing the guy from the record, which was less special than it should have been. I didn't care that it sounded different, I wanted it better. He played the song I wanted to hear most but it wasn't the same in the dark theater without my imagination's balloon.

The date got closer and the lineup evolved. No Dylan, yes Hendrix and Jefferson Airplane. There were some favorites, some losers and some that we'd never heard of. That wasn't an issue. There were so many great bands out there, all saying something different and never repeating themselves. You could go to someone's house and they put on a record that sucked, but the average was high enough that when someone said "you gotta hear this" it didn't make you cringe or want to run away.

It started on Friday but we left Woodstock (the town) on Thursday afternoon for the trip. We were in three cars, the Oldsmobile, a 1955 Chevy and a big fat DeSoto. We connected four hours later when we got to the festival grounds and set up in the first available camping space. We could have gotten closer but needed to get out of the car right away.

We set up in a meadow near to a power pole which would become a beacon so we'd know how to get back to the camp. Rudy told us there would be three daily meals. Breakfast at eight a.m. or when we got up. Lunch around noon and dinner around six; otherwise we were on our own. I never made it back for mealtimes and didn't know if Rudy did either.

I didn't care about the food, but my eleven-year-old sister, Julie had a different view. We were told that we would be treated with steaks and other nourishments, while the food bag was full of candy. Even a little girl with a sweet tooth knew that wasn't a good thing.

I started a ten-minute walk on crowded trails to scope out the stage. It wasn't quite finished but people were already sitting down in front waiting for the music to start. The day of the show settled about two hundred feet up the hill, where the crowd had started to thin out. I was on top of a small hill that looked down to the stage. The hill dipped down and up again, creating an area with an obstructed view. During the show several people settled in to the area behind me but left when they found they couldn't see anything. Right before Ravi Shankar, the last straggler moved out of the dip, and it was empty the rest of the night. It was a comfortable place to settle as long as you didn't care about seeing the stage.

We bought advance tickets but didn't use them as it became a free show. But I read and memorized everything on the ticket, including a lengthy warning that neither pets nor liquor would be allowed and breaking either directive would get you kicked out. There were quite a few dogs in attendance, so the first rule was gone. Compliance with the second rule was an accident. Liquor was not part of the equation back then, either because it was too heavy to carry, made you pee or was an "establishment" symbol. Woodstock's success was simple: People weren't drunk. They were eating stuff that made them peaceful, instead of combining it with something that brought out their belligerence.

During the festival itself neither the past nor the future existed. I was in the middle of the moment. An experience occurred, at its end I would move on to the next one. I looked forward to certain bands and wasn't so excited about others, but listened to everyone. I watched and listened, enjoyed or didn't, for the most part I didn't mourn the end of the last band or anticipate what was going to happen next. Except until around ten p.m. Sunday, when I started to lose steam and wondered where the fuck Crosby, Stills, Nash and Young were and why I had to sit through Blood, Sweat and Tears, Ten Years After, The Band and Johnny Winter. Was it worthwhile? Absolutely. It sounded great until the movie came out the following March and I heard the awkward dissonance of "Suite: Judy Blue Eyes."

There was an announcement: "The flat blue acid is poison." In the movie, the warning is for brown acid and the message is less incendiary and definitive. I can't swear they were passing out brown acid, or brown rice, but went along when a guy told me to open my mouth and threw in a small pill shaped like a barrel.

Sunrise stripped away my sensory filters. Everything rushed in at once. Hendrix arrived, dressed in white. He strolled up to the mike and said, "We meet again"—a reference to his appearance in Monterey two years earlier. As was the practice then, the majority of his set was either unreleased or unfamiliar. Not that it mattered. The stuff I knew I didn't really recognize due to the drugs and the noise.

I had expected Hendrix to be a towering figure, one who would dwarf everyone around him with his sheer size and cosmic weight. Before the set I kept picking out tall guys with frizzy hair that turned out to be someone else. He just appeared onstage, I must have blinked, and he seemed almost tiny. He was slender all around, especially his hands, which flew over the fretboard. I looked at my own hands, which were soaking in inferiority.

He talked in nonsense rhyme, going off on verbal tangents and ending every little speech with "blah blah woof woof."

But I knew exactly what he was talking about. He was speaking to me directly. Never mind all of the other people.

At the end of the festival I stood rooted to a spot at the top of the hill overlooking what held thousands of people hours before. It was littered with trash, sleeping bags and the detritus that a crowd leaves behind. Bob Dylan's "Desolation Row" was rolling around in my head.

It was my strongest defining moment up until then, and was something I would remember with awe for the rest of my life. However long that might be was up for grabs, because there was no sense of time.

 Since the Woodstock Festival oc- curred before everyone had a camera in their pocket its memories are crystallized through the efforts of just a few lucky and prescient professional shooters. Some of Elliott Landy's shots have become iconic representations of the event. Here (above) Landy catches a lone attendee making an unsafe scaffold climb in order to get a better view and (below) illustrating the frustration of festival goers who were stuck in the weather. Amateur shots (at left), this from then 18-year-old attendee Nancy Leith, were never shared widely and provide private treasures for those aware enough to bring along their Instamatics.

Tantalized

IN THE WEEKS FOLLOWING THE festival occupied my thoughts, dreams and speech. I drove people crazy with endless nattering of the coolness that I had witnessed. I found out quickly that much of the world was somewhat less impressed. Beginning with my own people. My cousin Paul, the ultimate source of all that was hip in our family, said he was on his way to the festival but turned back because of the crowds. He'd been in the middle of it all for several years, later calling the event "the beginning of the end."

My own sister, Julie, was something of a Woodstock casualty. She had gone to the festival along with Rudy and the rest of the camp but spent much of the time huddled in the tent. As soon as the car door opened I hit the ground running, in pursuit of girls, drugs and music. A little sister was the last thing on my mind. I didn't realize my rudeness until forty-eight years later when I sought her recollections about the festival.

After I ditched her the camp "counselor" did the same, going off to a swimming hole they said was "too muddy" for kids. This hurt at the time, but when she later saw pictures of naked swimming she was grateful for the protection against embarrassment.

Julie walked around some, but didn't really hear or see any of the performances. This was sealed on the second night, when she left a candle burning to let the counselor know she was there. It burned down to the end of the wick, and she awoke to find that her glasses had melted. So every time I asked "Did you see…" I was reminded of the stupidity of the question.

The experience wasn't all painful or negative. It was where she saw a naked man for the first time and she was intrigued by the energy. There was something going on there, even if she didn't know what it was. And weeks later, when she entered the sixth grade, none of her classmates knew about Woodstock, or cared.

Not me. I was in my first year of high school, on one side of the dividing line of people who went to Woodstock and people who didn't. It was all I could think about, or talk about, so any social capital earned by my presence was beaten to death by repetitive reminiscing.

It was mid-morning of a new era, where the world was experiencing a new wave of peace, love, sunshine and honesty. Everyone with long hair was a friend, sharing and interacting positive energy. It was us against everybody else.

Some people with long hair seemed untrustworthy, but we gave them the benefit of the doubt. That was, until we got home and found the grass we bought was catnip. Figuratively and literally. A long-haired guy named Charles Manson and his minions committed a series of murders in Los Angeles. So the hair rules no longer applied.

Truth became a casualty, especially when it came to attendance at Woodstock. "I was there," I might say. "So was I," said another. "Didn't see you there," I would answer jokingly as they acted as if they had been caught stealing. There was no proof either way, unless your face ended up in news coverage of the event or in the movie that came seven months later.

We were all connected through an underground grapevine that carried unverified information at the speed of sound. In late 1969 we heard on the radio about a planned Beatles performance at the Baltimore Civic Center. We were in the basement of someone whose older sister knew someone in the promoter's office who had just gotten her front-row seats for the Rolling Stones.

So I entered that house not knowing about the theoretical concert and left two hours later with imaginary front-row seats.

The Woodstock legend grew exponentially, through books, music, film and discussion. Even with this plethora of information there was still much left for discovery. This continues today, with reissues of live Woodstock sets and examination of the phenomenon at each significant anniversary. Five, ten, fifteen, twenty... Along the way the festival no longer only belonged to the people who attended, but everyone who wanted to share part of the experience.

I was working in Carlsbad, New Mexico ten years on, writing a column about the experience in retrospect. It gave me a chance to repeat my one profound original thought, that people got along at Woodstock because they were smoking pot and dropping acid, with nary a drop of alcohol to be found.

At twenty years I had moved to Oregon and recently married. *The Oregonian* declined my offer of a reminisce, but asked to borrow my copy of the free program that I had still held close. As time went on I forgot to pick it up and, at that point, didn't really care. Ten years after I was still in Oregon, writing about personal technology, and the Woodstock idea was antithetical to my life. The anniversary passed without notice.

Even if it was not front of mind it was still a defining moment. In between the two dates I worked the Woodstock idea into a freelance piece to the *Chicago Tribune* about the connection of technology and music.

In 2019, those who observe the 50th-anniversary Woodstock celebration from the comfort of their own homes probably will have the richer experience. After strapping on special goggles and sitting amid surrounding speakers, they will be able to use a home computer to select three-dimensional representations of different events as they occur, combined with authentic images from the past and speculative ones from the future. Through hand and eye motion, they will be able to change the pace and continuity as they edit out or repeat sequences at will.

It will be far different from the original concert in 1969, when most participants were overwhelmed and confused by the variety of experiences. Or last summer's festival, where concertgoers may have known what to expect but had to choose between two stages with no easy path from one to the other. The remote "participants" at the third festival, however, will be able to absorb everything. Video and audio from different sources will allow them to construct and create artificial surroundings that reflect a momentary mood and a particular preference.

Beyond Woodstock, the music community is buzzing with the possibilities of interactivity. It can become an extension of the popular boxed set, adding video, still photography and interviews to paint a portrait of the artist. It can be a game. It can add new experiences to an old album. It can become a showcase for new music or a way to present videos. Or it can blend all of this to come up with something new and different.

At the fortieth anniversary, I had escaped marriage from a woman with whom I did not share cultural values, whose idea of a 1969 defining moment was the moon landing. There was a bigger media splash, with *The New York Times* soliciting homemade videos from festival attendees. It wasn't the first time they had sent me a rejection note.

So I turned it into a mini-blog, in five chapters:

Repackaging's not what it used to be

Eight months after the festival there was a movie, and a soundtrack. Soon enough there was a second soundtrack. Home video evolved, and there was a cassette version and a videodisc. A video of "lost performances" followed, along with an extended version. DVDs after that, which brings us more or less to this year's fortieth-anniversary commerce-fest.

The fortieth anniversary was commemorated by a new version of the film, in regular and deluxe packaging. Both soundtracks will be reissued as they were, followed by a CD version that tracks the festival in a linear fashion, from Richie Havens's opener to Jimi Hendrix's finale. Along with this, five artists have released archival packages, each with their landmark 1969 album paired with a recording of their Woodstock appearance. Fans of Jefferson Airplane, Janis Joplin, Johnny Winter, Santana and Sly & the Family Stone will treasure these packages, even if they have heard the album hundreds of times before.

These sets satisfy the ultimate purpose of repackaging: to present old music in an appealing new light. This is either a public service for people who want to rediscover their faves, or a cynical play to sell the music one more time. Where a particular item falls on this sliding scale is directly related to whether you want it, or not.

And where you were when it happened. Those of us who attended the festival guarded the memory of the event, until we learned that it really didn't belong to us alone. The legend grew, into a space where all the memories were shared. It really didn't matter who was really there, and who stayed home. Today, the people who are most stimulated by the idea of Woodstock weren't even born then.

The original festival lost tons of money and the producers have been milking it ever since. This has resulted in a steadily annoying series of trashy products, although this new wave of stuff is of high quality. They match the posh coffee-table books and historical memorabilia that stock our bookstores and websites.

In modern times, everything from the Birth of Christ to the Civil War gets a posh historical package. It's appropriate that Woodstock gets the same treatment, even as it serves to further build the myth. It's a lock that people will discover more information, details and recollections just in time for the fiftieth anniversary in 2019.

What really happened, and didn't

I lived in the town of Woodstock as a child, which is not where the festival was held. Still, the little burg has benefited from the association and has built a substantial tourist empire as a result.

On a recent trip I bought a few souvenirs, including a refrigerator-magnet reproduction of the "original" festival ticket. Or so I thought. Once on the refrigerator it radiated some seriously uncool vibes. It listed the start time for each day as ten a.m., and I distinctly remembered that the first day kicked off several hours later than the other two. This was verified by the original festival poster, which states the first day started at four p.m., and the others at one p.m. So the ticket, while a quaint keepsake, was incorrect.

In 2009, I bought the deluxe limited edition of the Woodstock movie, which at the Costco price of forty-five dollars cost two and a half times the ticket's face value. The box set has a cute little iron-on patch, and a leather fringe trim representing the particularly obnoxious (and prohibitively expensive, at least for me) fashion that was big in those days. There is a copy of the *Life* magazine special edition, a very cool curio that would have been even better if they had managed to include the original advertising. Also contained is a ticket facsimile, that repeats the wrong times listed on my refrigerator version.

I can't argue that the time on the tickets or the color of the acid makes a lick of difference. It is the spirit of the gathering that sustains, from my memories and through all the subsequent repackages of the movie and the event. Even with all this profiteering, it's still clear this was one heck of a paradigm-shifter.

But you still wonder. If these little details are wrong, how many of the big ones are also incorrect? When you watch a Civil War documentary based on exhaustive research, how many of those details are based on erroneous souvenirs? Could some nineteenth-century entrepreneur have made a bogus misprint of Abe Lincoln's theater ticket, and he was actually assassinated on April 12?

In this case, the only important fact, like it says in all versions of the movie, is that a large group of people met for three days of peace and music and had nothing but three days of peace and music. But one day someone could get careless with the facts and the whole house of cards could tumble down.

The ticket's 'other' secret

The Woodstock Festival is renowned for its free environment and magical character, but there were some rules. As proof, the ticket facsimiles distributed as part of the new Woodstock box set provide a fascinating little detail when turned over. It is a lengthy warning that tells attendees that neither pets nor liquor would be allowed, and that breaking either directive would be grounds for ejection. There were quite a few dogs in attendance.

If Woodstock gave the generational light, the months-later Altamont festival provided a darker option. Held at a California racetrack just four months after Woodstock, it had some significant differences. It was a free show from the beginning, and the security was provided by a motorcycle gang. The Rolling Stones were the headliners, in the first tour since a three-year performance hiatus. Most significantly, there was a lot of liquor at Altamont.

So amid all this philosophizing about the beginning of the end (Woodstock) and the end of the beginning (Altamont) it became clear the secret to Woodstock's success was simple: People weren't drunk. Sometimes when the analyzing is over and all cultural generalities have been cast around for decades, the obvious truth emerges. Here, people were ingesting a substance that made them peaceful, instead of combining it with something that brought out their belligerence—as they learned to do, all too quickly.

A Better View Each Time

Up until now and presumably into the future, Woodstock content has populated every digital platform. Read this aloud. Don't those words just roll off your tongue? Back then, when your attendance at concerts was actually required, you needed to plan ahead and get to the venue early in order to get a good view, and there was no guarantee that some dancing hairball wouldn't jump in to block your view.

There were real rewards, like seeing Jimi Hendrix from thirty feet away, but we had to make a lot of sacrifices to get there. Today, you get the best view by staying home and watching taped concerts on a flat screen. It lacks certain atmosphere, but this is balanced by close proximity to the bathroom and the refrigerator.

The Woodstock reissues offer more diverse views of the performers than 90 percent of the original audience. The new version of the movie, actually a scrubbing of the "Director's Cut" of a few years back, has a couple of extra hours of "unseen" footage. The best of these are Johnny Winter and Paul Butterfield, people who were prominent at the time but never used the Woodstock momentum to get real fame, like Santana or Joe Cocker. These are great, because they are unexpected. Watching the movie on DVD at home is better than at the theater; you can speed ahead over the boring stuff or watch the favored sequences repeatedly.

Here is another place where the new clips shine: The songs are presented in their entirety, with no cutting and pasting of documentary footage. Watching the movie today, you notice that it is a good twenty minutes before a performance is shown. This is a bit too participatory for my tastes, as it recalls that much of any rock festival is time spent waiting. Recreating this in a movie really isn't all that enjoyable. We've known for some time that the whole festival was captured on tape and film, and that some of the results are pretty dreadful. Somewhere, there is still a motherlode of stuff, and some of it might even be pretty good. Some of what they've released on this go-round is actually pretty good, but you wonder how long it will take to get the whole story. Or if by the time it happens the only people who care will be obsessive, dead or both.

This time out, some of the dreadful stuff has been polished up. Participating musicians have visited the studio to redo their parts. When they are not available, their children have pitched in. This trend will continue with an expanded circle, since the people who are offended by this practice will die off. One day last week I put the Jimi Hendrix Woodstock DVD on the computer, popped on the headphones and watched it from thirty inches away. It was breathtaking, and wonderful for the senses. With everything said about Hendrix, the most rewarding experience is still watching him play.

After about four songs I stood up, brushed my teeth and played with the cat. It was nice to spend a few moments in the past, but I wouldn't want to live there full-time.

So many versions, so little time

An online search for "Woodstock Set List" provides differing results. Take the official version, from the Woodstock website. This is incorrect at least twice, since Mountain appeared on Saturday. Tim Hardin also played more than just two songs, but no one can say for sure which ones. The upcoming box set supposedly contains a complete set list, but with no accuracy guarantees.

Currently, the best published set list I have found is www.rockfiles.co.uk/ RockFiles_files/Woodstock.htm, although it repeats the Hardin error. But it earns high marks for its inclusion of "Master Mind" in Jimi Hendrix's set.

This was a song by his backing guitarist, Larry Lee. At the time I wondered why Hendrix allowed Lee the song, since it was of such lower quality than the rest of the set. Ultimately I admired Hendrix's generosity, and respected him all the more. (There is no actual recording of "Master Mind," only an indication that it existed. And to go slightly off topic, the mostly complete recording of Hendrix's set still is and always will be the best recorded document of the festival.)

The new versions add to the several different iterations of the festival's soundtrack; none are complete. This isn't a bad thing. I challenge any festival attendee's assertion that every note was worthwhile, and they enjoyed everything they heard. Tastes were diverse. Some people loved the Jefferson Airplane and hated the Grateful Dead, and vice versa. I sat through Ten Years After, The Band, Blood, Sweat and Tears and Johnny Winter in a bad mood, waiting anxiously for Crosby, Stills, Nash & Young. Was it worthwhile? Listen to the awkward, dissonant version of "Suite: Judy Blue Eyes" and decide for yourself, and compare it with recordings of Winter's electric twelve-string cacophony.

The new version of the soundtrack, due in August, is remarkable for a few reasons. It is arranged sequentially, with a song or two from every artist in playing order (note Mountain in the Saturday sequence). Due to copyright issues, only three artists are missing: The Band, Ten Years After and the (then, as today) unknown Keef Hartley Band. None of this makes sense. The Band participated in the late 1990s repackage, and Ten Years After's "I'm Going Home" is found on all versions of the original soundtrack; first released in 1970 and in a new version this year.

CBS offshoot Legacy Records is featuring five of its artists in its "Woodstock Experience" series. Jefferson Airplane, Janis Joplin, Santana, Sly & the Family Stone and Johnny Winter all get the treatment. It includes a copy of an album released that year, along with a recording of their Woodstock show; presumably in its entirety. These packages are all flawed, since a lot of the music is either clumsy or dated. Still, it provides a warts-and-all portrait of each artist, and becomes an honest keepsake of the time. Too many reissues are rewrites or whitewashes of history; these present the old wine in a slightly new bottle without changing the taste.

For the truly diverse, all five sets are available in a single package. These new products complement what is already available on the 25th Anniversary Package, the original soundtrack and its sequel. You will need to dig a bit here to find which rarities exist and are important. I can't cross-check everything, but there are several worthwhile and unique tracks in this particular library. For instance, the Woodstock recording of Neil Young's "Sea of Madness" is a nice little pop tune that, prior to its inclusion on Young's pricey new "Archives" set, is only available on a Woodstock album.

With these new packages you can buy them all and go long, or you can focus on the best stuff and leave the rest to the ages.

———

June 9, 2015

By the time I got to the Woodstock Museum it was nearly half past noon. I felt a sharp uptick from the pot candy I'd swallowed during the ride over. It wasn't quite the same as a time forty-six years earlier, when a surprise tab of acid from

a stranger launched me thirty feet away from Jimi Hendrix, swearing I would never pick up a guitar again. I've told that story for years and no one believes it anymore.

Here and now, on the porch outside of the museum on the site of the original festival, watching a Montessori field trip trickle by, on their way to an auditorium where they can hear about the protest movement. I've already done the museum, the gift shop, and walked the concert

Where it happened

site, which includes a memorial plaque, a banged-up tract of mud where the stage used to be, and a giant peace sign carved into the side of a hill, accomplished by mowing one area of grass two inches lower than the rest of the field.

The field was a lot smaller than I imagined or remembered. It was a big hill, certainly, but how did 450,000 people ever fit here?

Those of us who attended the festival guarded the memory of the event until we learned that it really didn't belong to us alone. The legend grew, into a space where all the memories were shared. It really didn't matter who was really there, and who stayed home. Today, the people who are most stimulated by the idea of Woodstock weren't even born at the time.

When I tell people that I was at Woodstock, the conversation stops and they look at me with awe. They ask for unknown details, although some try to trip me up and prove I was there. I try not to drag it on too long, since attending Woodstock was more of a chance occurrence than an accomplishment.

Hearing my story, people ask if it really happened. As time goes on, I'm not so sure.

Tactlessness/1

———

Serious fandom prompts people to chip off their own little sliver of a celebrity's life, to bask in its glow and show it to their friends. This process isn't always frivolous, as some people pursue connections with Bill Gates or the Dalai Lama instead of the Kinks or the Kardashians.

Many people are satisfied observing an event and going home afterwards. Others seek more, be it yelling for encores or attempting to gather a unique experience through personal interaction. It is at those times they act silly, walking away with a memory that makes them appear less than brilliant. But at least they have a souvenir.

1970

May 31, 1970; Washington DC

You awake feeling empty, even though the previous night should have filled you up. Crosby, Stills, Nash and Young live, finally, for the second time. As soon as they left the Woodstock stage you knew you needed to see them again. It nearly happened two months later at Constitution Hall, but that was canceled when Crosby's girlfriend died in a car crash.

You felt for her—and for Crosby— but wondered why he didn't just carry on, because these things happen all the time. Mark Kinsey's sister died last year and he was back in class two days later.

It was as remarkable a show that could ever occur, but you had trouble focusing. You found the seat and made a bathroom run, once seated you still had to pee. You couldn't get over the fact that you were actually there enough to enjoy the music, although you relaxed when Crosby said they would "play all night." You had time to adjust. But it seemed a bit rude when they slunk off the stage one hundred and fifty minutes later.

You got a chance to pee during a slow Nash piano song, were there and back before the song ended. It was a great to hear familiar songs performed but was greater to hear new songs performed for the first time. Young was the best, with "Don't Let It Bring You Down" and "Southern Man," although you weren't sure about the titles. There was a new political song called "Ohio" and they ended with an a cappella refrain. Something about freedom.

It was over before it happened. You perked up when Nash said "we'll see you at Emergency tomorrow," referring specifically to the downtown club that had become the center of Georgetown, at least from your perspective.

On the way home you discovered that Scott and Dave didn't hear it in the same way.

"He was saying there was urgency because we need to end the war tomorrow," Scott said.

You aren't convinced. Dave's interpretation was less likely: "There is an insurgency and they're riding around in a wheelbarrow."

They went back and forth like that for a while, you stopped listening. They knew each other since grade school, but you had just met them this year. You were riding up with them for a few dollars' worth of gas and three joints, which were smoked in succession before the show. You wished there was some left right now.

"You can't think they are going anywhere near Emergency anytime soon," Dave said. "When word got out the place would be jammed with people and you won't even be able to breathe. They'll start a riot."

Which is why, you told yourself, it was important to get there early.

The next morning you pretend to forget that mowing the lawn was part of the deal that allowed you to attend the show. There is something going on downtown, you say, and begin the trek.

The bus drops you off at the end of Wisconsin Avenue. You walk east on M toward Emergency as fast as you can without knocking anyone over. After two blocks it doesn't seem to make a difference since the sidewalk crowd thins to a handful. You were expecting crowds, maybe they were already inside. So you pick up the pace.

Getting closer to the Emergency, you could see a few people lined up but it was for a movie at the movie theater next door. You still hurried up to the Emergency with no one outside so you flung open the door and walked inside, only to immediately go blind from the darkness.

There was no balance between the bright sun and the club. It had a narrow hall leading to a larger room in back with stage, seating and a dance floor, where you headed in order to see who might be setting up in secret. There was no one, and it was completely dark. You pretended to use the bathroom and walked nonchalantly toward the front where the guy in charge today was reading a copy of *Woodwind*.

"Who's playing today?" you ask, and follow with "Where is everybody?" That earns you a pitying glance.

"No one," he says. "Obviously. There was some big concert in Baltimore last night so people are either sleeping or they're at Dupont Circle. Why would you want to be inside today, anyway?"

You leave without a word, turning left on M Street toward Dupont Circle and walking swiftly to where Nash and his friends are certainly playing to an eager crowd.

After a block you slow down, then stop short and turn around. You realize it will take twenty minutes to walk ten blocks, only to find that Nash had either come and gone or more likely never planned to be there in the first place.

You realize that fourteen hours after the concert ended, it was really over. There wouldn't be any more encores or replays. You turn around and head home, walking backwards with your thumb out because it's too much effort to stand still on a corner or at a bus stop.

Hitchhiking through DC is usually easy but sometimes the luck runs out when you cross the Maryland line. Today you are dropped off at River Road and Western Avenue, which isn't exactly on the way home. You accepted the ride that took you there because you wanted to talk about the concert with someone, although you did not disclose the details of your recent unsuccessful scavenger hunt.

You are standing there for ten minutes, then fifteen. There are more cars on Wisconsin Avenue but you aren't sure how far that is. You begin to hum the ride mantra "A ride, a ride, please I need a ride, a ride, a ride, please I need a fucking ride" to the tune of "Heigh Ho, Heigh Ho..." with no success. Maybe you didn't wait long enough before asking for help. Or maybe it was because you were now standing in a bus stop in an attempt to hedge your bets.

You can usually tell when someone will stop before it happens. Anyone with long hair will always pull over and even cross lanes to help even if they are only going a short way, while crewcuts will usually pass by staring straight ahead. Old people in their forties never stop unless it's your parents or the parents of some longhair and they know how it feels. It's good this doesn't happen a lot because you never know what to say to these people.

Finally someone pulls over. A guy and a girl in a white Chevy convertible. You wouldn't expect them to stop but times are changing. Or maybe not.

"Oh, sorry," he says. "I thought it was a girl." The real girl laughs.

You flip, reliving all the times some short-haired asshole has brought misery into your life over the past few years, how their menace makes you cringe in fear every time a leather jacket walks by. How you could never go to the pizza parlor because that's where they hung out and you had to pretend you didn't really like pizza. How the prettiest girls won't talk to you even though you can see they want to, because their friends would make fun of them. And you can tell they all really want to talk to you.

You remember all of the adults who look at you with a sneer but are too polite to say anything, and those who forbade you to hang around with their kids because you are a bad influence (increasingly inconvenient since the kids supplied you with grass and you always had to find a new source). That you just hallucinated a show, running madly across town for an event that never had the remotest chance of actually taking place.

You flip him the bird.

He is pulling out when he sees it in the mirror and plants the car in the middle of the bus stop. He gets out and charges, spitting in your face and grabbing you by the arm. It was rude what you did, he screamed, and you need to apologize. If his wife wasn't here he would kick the shit out of you, he said. And he still might.

You say, "I apologize," which increases his heat.

"Not to me, to her."

You turn to the girl seeing her for the first time. She has a pinched expression and a scarf wrapped around her hair that appears to be in curlers.

"I apologize," you say again.

"That was pretty rude," she says and turns her eyes away.

Rude. What's really rude is how your stupid little-mustache husband needs to show off in front of you by picking on people half his size and one-quarter inclined to fight back. That he finds it necessary to pull over and offer the hope of getting a ride out of this godforsaken neighborhood and then yanking it away. That he acts all tough and manly when it's clear that the only thing he really wants to do is suck your dick.

Speaking these thoughts would not be a good thing.

"I apologize," you say a third time. "It won't happen again."

———

June 29, 1970; Columbia, MD

The Who was loud and kinetic, three whirling dervishes and a fourth who moved nothing but his fingers that you ended up watching most of the time. A lot of adrenaline here. You were part of the rush crowd that ended up in the orchestra pit, and had a pretty close view.

But it was something of a disappointment. You had read interviews where Pete Townshend talked about the new music the band would play on the tour, and there was a final performance of *Tommy* in New York in the early spring. So you were primed for something new and exciting.

You'd seen them twice in the past year and were used to the routine. They began with a noisy song by bassist John Entwistle, the magic-fingered bassist, following it with a selection of covers and originals. Familiar and not.

Tommy was always the middle third of the show; you expected they would play the new stuff in the same slot.

Instead you got *Tommy*. Again.

They played their regular set, half of which you didn't really like that much. It wasn't boring, since watching these four was always fun. Bassist Entwistle's fingers. Townshend wearing the same white jumpsuit as when you saw them in November, except with paint stains. Roger Daltrey's lariat microphone which always made you flinch when it swung over your head. There was tape about an inch thick between the microphone and the wire, but it was still scary. Keith Moon, the drummer, would throw his sticks in the air and have a new pair with the next beat.

Then it was over. You wanted more and walked toward backstage, which was bordered with a medium-height chain-link fence. Stage right looked pretty deserted, a good place to sneak in. If that didn't work you'd have to go to the other side where there was a guard and a gate.

You end up following a guy on crutches. You both saw a gate, which to your surprise was unlocked. You thought he was about to let you in, instead he turns around, pushes you to the ground with his crutch and locks the gate.

Dusting yourself off you head for the other side, where a pair of brothers were begging the guy at the gate to let them in.

A few months earlier the family cat was neutered. Instead of putting the license tag on her collar you attached a string and wore it around your neck. At a particularly exciting point in the show, you tossed the tag toward the stage where it landed without anyone noticing.

It was now in the hands of the gate guard.

"I'll tell you what," he said. "If you can tell me what's on there I'll let you in."

"That's mine," you say, snatching it away. Dumb move. You should have let it play out. Quick recovery. "It says 'Montgomery County Animal Hospital.'"

The gate guy didn't seem to realize the backward sequence.

"OK then," he said. "Go on in."

People were milling around, there were some huge trucks waiting and a picnic table full of food. You look around wondering where to go, when one brother pointed out a set of metal stairs and said, "They come out over there."

Which they did, about ten minutes later. They were taking their time, heading slowly toward the trucks. You walk up to Entwistle.

"Do you lose your hearing for a while, after a show like that?" you ask.

"No," he said.

"You were great up there."

"Thank you."

Daltrey strolls by.

"Don't your ears trouble you?" you ask.

He repeats the question slowly.

"Not really," he said and walked away.

Townshend was standing next to a blue car holding a paper cup and talking to a shorter guy who was wearing horn-rims.

"Can I have a sip of your Coke?" you say to Townshend. Not waiting for an answer, you take the cup out of his hand and take a drink. A foul taste.

"It's beer," he said and continued his conversation with Horn-Rims.

You hand it back to him and stepped back a few inches. Townshend kept talking as if you weren't ever there. Which you really weren't.

Pete Townshend just gave me my first sip of beer, you thought. *I nearly spat it out, and now I feel like an idiot.*

Theatrical

———

Part of wanting to get closer to the music and musicians led to the idea that you might some day meet them and kiss them on the lips. Girls had it easy; they could pick any number of cute performers as a crush object. They were defined by their crushes. Someone who swooned over Davy Jones of the Monkees offered a different challenge than one who favored Eric Burdon of the Animals. And young girls who did not have a crush object were somehow less cool.

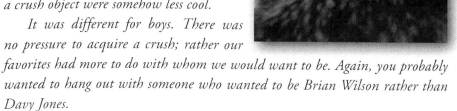

It was different for boys. There was no pressure to acquire a crush; rather our favorites had more to do with whom we would want to be. Again, you probably wanted to hang out with someone who wanted to be Brian Wilson rather than Davy Jones.

Sooner or later, boys would see someone who rang their bell. There weren't a lot of crush-worthy female singers. Cher? Jackie DeShannon? Not really strong personalities. Joan Baez wasn't an option. So little boys turned to actresses. After a brief dalliance with Sally Field, who sent me a machine-autographed picture when I wrote a letter protesting the cancellation of Gidget, I settled on Diana

Rigg. She was elusive, appearing on a show that was impossible to find for any length of time. She was tough and witty and challenging. "Pretty" can be commonplace.

Both boys and girls outgrew these crushes with the option of actual physical contact. We all looked fondly back, and then followed their progress. Down the line some people had the opportunity to meet their crushes and say how much they meant. Which in most cases was also the opportunity to say something really stupid.

————

February 11, 1975

I saw Diana Rigg onstage in *The Misanthrope* last night and had no real idea of what was going on. The play was written by Moliéré in the sixteen-hundreds as a French parlor drama and updated to a modern look and a new location, Scotland. I know all that from reading the program, as I didn't comprehend a whole lot. It may as well have been Shakespeare, or French.

There's a grumpy guy who hates everyone, but Diana Rigg—whatever her character was—is in love with him. He loves her too but can't abide her habits. For me it wasn't about the play, instead I watched the stage and thought. "Wow, that's really her."

When I was eleven years old she became my celebrity crush, something I perceived with disdain in girls my age. There was a jealousy element, because these girls lavished more attention on imaginary George Harrison than on real-life me.

I got to know Rigg as a monochrome image on a ten-inch TV shared by the whole family. The show was *The Avengers*, a spy drama with a sense of humor. I didn't notice how Diana Rigg and John Steed managed so stay so suave and debonair while facing deadly situations.

Her role on the *Avengers*, Emma Peel, fit nicely into the secret-agent worship of the time, so she could step into my fantasy life without missing a beat. She was also British, which was only fitting. Girls my age carried on about British rock stars, so it made sense that I would latch on to a British actress. Especially since the only female British rock stars were Lulu and Dusty Springfield, neither were particularly exciting.

Rigg had depth. She stimulated the mind as well as the eye, a sex symbol with intellectual appeal. I never succumbed to the idea of a media romance and never thought I was "in love" with her. However, she became my idea of the perfect woman—beauty, brains, charm and independence.

Part of it was that most people didn't know her, so I kind of had her to myself. But there were a few of us around. When we moved to DC I met a few people with a similar worship, and it brought us closer.

Once *The Avengers* ended she turned up in the strangest places. First it was *On Her Majesty's Secret Service*, a James Bond movie starring someone who wasn't Sean Connery. I actually never saw it, and still haven't. Then she turned up in *The Hospital* as a free spirit, which was cool because I didn't know she was in the movie and it was a big surprise when her name appeared in the opening credits. She was in most of the movie, and I spent that time thinking "Wow, that's Diana Rigg," rather than following the plot. Kind of like at the play.

Year before last she had her own half-hour comedy show which I eagerly anticipated, but stopped watching after three disappointing episodes. The only memorable moment was when she, as a fashion designer, got in a tiff with Philip Proctor, who was in Firesign Theater and playing her boss while sitting on a stool. When he stood he was a foot shorter than she was. It was the only time I laughed.

Theatre of Blood was a treat, though. Vincent Price played an over-the-top actor who was doling out Shakespearean deaths to those who criticized him or stood in the way of his career. Rigg played his daughter, an active participant in the mayhem.

Seeing her was always cool, although much of my thoughts gravitated to the fact that I was seeing her and not on what she was doing.

———

February 25
If craziness were electricity I'd be a fucking generator. I have actually done what I've threatened to do for weeks and requested time in the court of Queen Diana.

Two days ago I went by the Kennedy Center's stage door, asking the guard when she usually arrived and departed. I thought he would guard this information, but he told me that she arrived at around six thirty and left sometime between ten and ten thirty.

Today I settled down for a nap right after lunch. When I woke up I was motivated. I sat right down and wrote her a letter, requesting an interview on behalf of my college paper.

> *We are the* Spur, *a college newspaper with a slightly freaked out staff and an eye for opportunity. The opportunity is, quite plainly, your illustrious presence in our humble town, and would be very honored if you would grant us a half-hour of your time for an informal, conversational interview.*

The letter was low on intellect and high on flattery, which I thought she would welcome since she is underappreciated in the States.

I finished the letter at around quarter after five. Couldn't decide whether to make a run for it or wait until tomorrow. This had happened a few times, where I'd started a letter, given it up and put it off until later. I decided to go ahead while I had the courage and motivation.

I drove Cabin John Parkway, Canal Road and down to the Kennedy Center, parking right outside of the stage door. It was around ten fifteen. I didn't have much time. I grabbed the letter and walked toward the door, almost colliding with her as she emerged.

"Ms. Rigg," I said, handing her the letter. "I work for my college paper and would like to interview you." She sort of smiled, took the letter and and said, "I will call you." I didn't believe that for a second, but at least I got to say hello. Which was a pretty good story, in and of itself.

I am an optimist and do believe in the possibility that my request will have positive results. I guess it's silly waiting around for the phone to ring, but I will jump every time it does.

February 27

My biggest fear was that she would call when I wasn't home and that Kurt, Jimmy or Gregg would take the message that she wasn't interested. They get all of the chicks. As it turned out, I came home today to find out I'd missed her call by ten minutes.

"Diana Rigg just called," Jimmy said, unsticking himself from the end of a bong. "She said you should be at the stage door at six p.m. Tuesday."

Jimmy, who can be a bit of a jerk, wasn't beyond a fakeout and knows how badly I want this. But he insisted, and I eventually decided that he was telling the truth. So I better start preparing. The worst thing is that I'll look stupid, which I will anyway.

———

March 4

It's done, and I'm all wired.

Since Thursday I've been making out lists of questions, asking what they would ask Diana Rigg if they had the opportunity. I wasn't really asking for a question, only bragging about my own opportunity. If anyone came up with something good it would be a bonus.

No luck either way. Maybe because I was asking guys. Half of them suggested a proposal, while others pursued a more pornographic path. "I'd ask her to marry me" devolved in "I'd ask her to fuck me." Which was offensive, as my crush was built on respect.

Pure or not, my crush has a sexual element and a strong physical and psychological pull. Tempered with realism. Realistically, there are several reasons that the crush will never be consummated. First off, she would need to be attracted to me, my body and mind, which will never happen. She's world-famous, or at least in my world. She's sixteen years older than I am, and lives elsewhere. She's already married to an Israeli artist. Take all that away, and there is the certainty that I would not be able to "perform" under those conditions.

As the possibility of a serious connection with her is impossible, improbable and insane I will admit that I want her to like me, be impressed by me, and continue some kind of friendship afterward.

I typed out a list of thirty-five questions, knowing that I wouldn't ask them all. When I took the two-page list out of my pocket and set it on the chair next to me, she must have wondered what on earth she had agreed to.

The plan was to go down the list and ask as many questions as possible until time ran out. But I shifted to a more random process, where I'd look for a question that was sort of connected to the one she was answering. I was only half-listening to her as I was focused on the next question. I was also amazed that I was there talking to her in person, which was a distraction that kept me out of the moment.

I began asking her about her musical tastes.

I use rock and soul all the time when I'm in the car or around the house. When I'm thinking or introspective I use classical music. Music shouldn't be used in the way that I use it, you should lend yourself to the music. I manipulate music as to what I need.

One of the themes here is how she has gone where no woman has gone before. She provided another example when I asked about her early days.

There is a tradition in the theater, that the lowest of the low is the "spear carrier." They are generally men, but I was the only female spear carrier. Like in Shakespeare, in a crowd scene, there is always someone carrying a spear or something, just standing there not doing anything. It's the fellows that do it generally, but because I was so tall I became a female spear carrier.

Not sure where this was going. I asked a question that I expected to lead up to later but it just popped out, how she felt about being a sex symbol.

I think it always helps. It's not something that I pursue myself. I'll never do pinup photographs, I'm incapable of taking them seriously. One is sexual and it's quite nice to be recognized as a sex symbol if you don't have to work at it. You know, the boredom of having your boobs jacked up. I don't go for that at all.

For the most part, the parts I've played haven't been blatantly sexual. Except for The Avengers, *which catered to every sexual appetite. Flagellation, the leather kick, the shoes, bondage. It was all there.*

If one wasn't admired one where one was in the sense that I wouldn't be playing the lead in a play. I wouldn't be offered parts. People buy tickets so they can see what you're doing.

The bad part is idolization, because I don't think I qualify to be idolized. I know too much about myself and I know plenty of people they can idolize, who are worthy of it. This is very much a twentieth-century sort of thing that has gathered momentum over the years in the entertainment industry. A lot of people in the entertainment industry allow it to happen and court it, pretending to be what they aren't. Thereby, they swell the ranks of the idolators.

This one is a bit confusing. "Boring" isn't the word I would use to describe breast enhancement. Perhaps the British have a different vernacular. And she played tennis with the tenses. *"If one wasn't admired … in the sense that I wouldn't be playing the lead in a play …people buy tickets so they can see what you're doing."*

I could refine her quotes to reflect what I think she meant but that would be dishonest. These quotes need to be pure and complete.

Watching her, I could see elements of every role she had played, none so strong to reflect her personality. She sure wasn't Emma Peel in real life.

Every role has an area you identify with, that's the part that's easiest. The most difficult part is delving into the area that you haven't lived, that you don't understand and is alien to you. But more or less, every well written part has a number of human qualities you can recognize in yourself.

I choose my roles out of sheer perversity. I've done a horror movie, I've done crappy bits and pieces of this, that and the rest of it. I did a failure of a TV series in California. I've done classic roles. I follow my appetite, that's all.

I asked questions, checking off the list. They didn't sound as smart as they did when I typed them out, and I was nervous. I'd ask a question and she wouldn't respond right away, so I asked it again or from a different direction. I wasn't sure if it was going well but the tape was running and I'd deal with it later. After a while it felt like it might be getting close to the end so I went with a quickie, asking why she had granted me the interview.

Because you're young, and you're beginning and because I'm bored with old jaded journalists asking a lot of fucking stupid questions, if you'll excuse my language … you've heard it before.

My instincts were correct, as a scratchy voice came over the intercom. "One half hour, one half hour please." She responded: "Well, that's about it." I switched off the tape, thanked her and found my way outside.

Walking into the setting sun's shine was a shock, increased by the emotional tightrope I'd balanced on for the last half hour.

I walked over to the edge of the outer walkway and looked across the river, talking to myself.

"I did it. I really fucking did it."

———

March 14

A lot has happened this week, Diana-wise. I spent Sunday at the paper's production facility in Silver Spring, reading the proof line by line. I don't trust anyone else on the staff to pay a lot of attention to this, since this is just another story to them. This is my first big interview, the one that will set the stage for what promises to be a successful career interviewing rock stars and actresses.

I needed to be careful and precise, and to cover all the topics discussed during the interview. Thursday, right after I calmed down, I stayed up all night and transcribed the tape, ending up with three single-spaced lowercase typo-ridden text. This took a long time, as every quote had to be correct. I couldn't have Diana reading the piece next week and thinking "That's not what I said."

A few typos slipped in, and the layout was disappointing. The article took all of Page 9, not the most prominent position. The picture, blurry and out of focus to begin with, didn't reproduce well. From what I can guess by one paragraph's words and measuring the piece it runs about 1,800 words. Pretty long, and I guess I shouldn't expect most people to read it all the way through.

I got to school early on Tuesday, all excited about getting a first copy, and read it all the way through several times. There already was a response, but not one that I had hoped for or expected.

"One of the drama people was just in here," said Chris, the editor. "She was pissed that we gave a whole page to Diana Rigg and didn't bother to review the latest school play."

I don't care, really. My purpose here is to contribute occasional pieces about the stuff I like. I'm not going to cover one school thing. There's nobody famous involved and it is impossible to guess who will be famous in the future.

This piece has its flaws, but deserves more than Page 9 in the Montgomery College *Spur-ious*. So I took the original fourteen pages and glued them together continuously into a scroll. I wrote a new opening that was about her and not me. I cut a lot of personal stuff, my observations, and toned down the idolatry. If I'm going to play in the big leagues I need to have a more streamlined game. It was wise to emphasize her quotes and downplay my ruminations.

I cut out the rejected prose, literally. An offending paragraph would be snipped out of the scroll and glued back together. I used a red pen to cross out some words and add some others. Next was retyping the draft on clean paper. I finally got it down to about nine pages. Long, but not what it was before.

The final draft included a variety of topics: *The Avengers*, stage, screen or TV, role selection, critics, personal value, friendship, idolization, spare time, anonymity, a sense of humor and cosmetic surgery. Maybe I'm too close to this but I couldn't figure out what to cut.

Where to go now? The *Post* and the *Star* both did long stories about her so that would be a no-sale. I think the best opportunity is with *Ms.* magazine, since they buy into the idea of feminine power and breaking down walls. I went to the library and found their listing in *Writer's Market*. It was optimistic, in that they bought freelance. Not so optimistic was the response time, four to six weeks, which I couldn't abide. The best option now becomes going to New York and dropping in so they have to pay attention. If I call first they will definitely say no.

———

March 24

It's been raining all morning, worse than yesterday. I'm in a bar, Beef and Burger at Broadway and 44th Street. It's a few blocks from Port Authority and the bus to DC but there's no rush. Between Greyhound and Trailways, buses leave every hour or so.

I'm tired, soaked and discouraged, as this little trip didn't work out quite as planned.

I arrived in New York for DC by bus yesterday. On the way up I scoured photocopies of several *Writer's Market* pages but didn't come up with any new leads. Is this a waste of time? Maybe, but it had already begun and I needed to follow through. There wasn't really a choice since I was already on the bus.

After leaving the bus station I walked to the *Ms.* office at 41st and Lexington Avenue. Inside, I saw my reflection in the gold-flecked wall covering. I looked pretty scary. If I saw me on the street I would go the other direction. But it had already begun.

I went in anyway. I looked pretty washed out, but so was everybody else today. I walked into the office at which time the receptionist—who didn't look too much older than me—offered the expected greeting.

"Can I help you?" she said.

"Yes, I'm a writer from DC and I've written a story about Diana Rigg that I hope you will publish," I said.

"You can give it to me and I'll pass it on. You should hear in about six weeks."

"Yes, I saw that. But I'll be out of the country then (a stretch, since my vacation was scheduled for early July) and was wondering if it was possible to speed things up a bit."

I knew right away this was on the edge of pushy. So I smiled to take that edge away.

"One minute," she said, and picked up the phone. After about thirty seconds she hung up and told me to have a seat.

Fifteen minutes later a woman came out of the big wooden doors, introduced herself as Judith Wilson, and sat next to me. She was black, with her natural hair cropped close. An interesting look, which you don't see much on women of any race. I wonder if it will catch on.

I said I was in town visiting family and wanted to drop the story off in the hope of making things go a little faster. I pulled myself back from pushy, saying that I didn't expect a decision right away.

She read the first few lines of the piece.

"I have some time this afternoon when I might be able to read this," she said. "You should come back tomorrow." Not as good as I wanted, but better than I expected. I thanked her and left.

I took my time walking to Nanny's apartment (65th and West End), arriving at around four p.m. She fussed over me. It was a bit annoying and intrusive. I wished she would just sit down and relax so I could tell her the Diana Rigg story without her asking me whether I wanted a cookie every five minutes. But we all play roles and I let it go.

The evening's plan was to go down to the St. James Theatre, around the corner from where I am now, and give Diana a copy of the story, published last week. I began walking the twenty blocks downtown, arriving at the stage door at around six forty-five. I thought that would give me enough time to give her a copy, have her scan a few words and maybe tell her about the *Ms.* opportunity.

You would think that a theater in New York would have more rules than one in DC. But when I told the guy at the door I was dropping something off for Diana Rigg, he told me to go right in. The backstage area was crowded so I stood against the wall. When someone asked, I told them the same thing as the guard.

"Wait right here," he said. "She's coming out of makeup and her dressing room is down the hall."

After about five minutes she arrived, moving quickly. She was wearing a robe and a bathing cap on her head, presumably to accommodate the wig. I called out, not identifying myself because she couldn't have forgotten me from two weeks ago. "I brought you a copy of my article," I said, holding it out.

She looked at me with silent shock. I handed her the paper. She took it, thanked me in a voice that said "go away," and went down the hall.

I walked back uptown, hitting Columbus Circle before I saw the truth. I wanted her to like me but that was never possible, especially now. She had given me the interview and that was it, as far as she was concerned. Tonight I had invaded her world, uninvited.

On Broadway I got a souvlaki sandwich, something that you can't get anywhere else than New York. I went back to Nanny's and she fussed some more. I slept on the fold- out bed, where you could feel the springs. Which I interpreted as torture deserved.

The next day I entered the *Ms.* office, only a little less scraggly than before. The receptionist pulled out an envelope and put it on the narrow space in front of her.

"Judith had an early meeting and asked that I give this to you when you came in," she said. I returned to the lobby, sat on the marble bench and opened the envelope, which included my manuscript and a handwritten-on-both-sides piece of *Ms.* memo paper.

This reads well enough to be published, but is missing a focus that makes it something that should be published in Ms.

I don't blame you if you don't feel like reading further. In case you do I'm adding a few quibbles with the piece regardless of where it eventually runs.

Maybe I came off a bit more egotistical than intended.

She wrote that the lead was "a bit weak" and doesn't grab the reader swiftly enough to pull the reader into the focus of the piece, that I might want to begin with a paragraph later in the piece about her innovations when it came to feminism.

She wrote that I should "slightly" reorganize the piece.

In case you are wondering what kind of piece about Diana Rigg would suit Ms., *I suspect it would be an interview focusing on the point you raise in the first sentence of your final paragraph (page 10). I don't think that the interview or the interviewer's comments would have to be confined exclusively to this question ("sex symbol" vs. "Versatile and talented actress"), in fact our readers would probably be bored stiff if it did. However, since this magazine is part of a movement to examine and reshape the image of women, the question of the nature of Ms. Rigg's popularity and her own view of her significance as a female performer is crucial to any piece that would appear in* Ms.

There is no way I'd get Diana to sit down for another interview, especially considering last night. I should probably give this one up and move on to the next thing. This whole thing wasn't a complete failure, but it succeeded only up to a point.

Her note is encouraging and welcome. The piece needs work but "reads well enough to be published." That she took the time to read it and provide a detailed response was a welcome change from the rejection slips I have gotten so far. Often pre-printed, their main message was that the piece did not fit their needs and they wished me luck in future endeavors. Making it clear that such endeavors will have nothing to do with them.

I've been sitting here for a while, postponing the trip while reading *Jaws* in paperback. Most likely I'll take a 1:00 bus so I'll get to Silver Spring in the daytime and won't have to hitchhike in the dark.

I closed my eyes for a minute, mini-dreaming that a famous person sat down with me and I couldn't figure out who she was. So I'm going to play with the idea for a while and write a fictional account of what didn't almost happen. For expediency I'll write about the first famous person that comes to mind. I think the school paper does something for April Fool's, so this will fit right in.

———

Dark Horseshit

By Abbie Rhoads

Outside it was a combination of snow wind and hail, or "snailing," as the waitress so astutely put it. Inside the jam-packed Beef & Burger at the corner of Broadway and 44th Street, I was virtually crying into my beer. I had spent all day running around the city trying to sell a story with no success, and was killing time before the next bus to DC.

When a natty guy with a tweed hat and a mustache accompanied by a slightly younger black man asked if they could join me at my booth I was more than eager for the company, if only to tell them my tale of woe. Not really looking at them, I barely recount of the events of the day, whining, what's a writer to do?

Afro ordered a Michelob while English asked for carrot juice. Carrot juice, really? For the first time I looked carefully at my companions, astounded that I had not recognized them immediately. I was sharing a table with George Harrison and Billy Preston.

Preston had left his trademark Afro home so he looked like any other guy. Harrison wore two buttons, the mantra OM and another saying WIN in capital letters. I recalled that President Gerald Ford had given Harrison that button, which stood for "Whip Inflation Now," during a White House visit last year.

"I know you are a journalist and they're such a nasty lot," George said to me. "So if you fancy writing anything about this we can just leave."

Please stay, I said, quickly assuring him that I would have liked to have been in a position to write a positive review of his last tour which I had seen just a few months ago. The tour was much-maligned by "nasty journalists," and I assumed this was the source of George's attitude.

I hastily added that I was a unique journalist because I wrote only nice things about people.

He softened, or seemed to.

"If I tell you something, will you promise to print it in your school paper only? I mean, reporters are so nosy and deceitful. I'll give you a chance but if you spread this around now you could jeopardize it. I'm fed up with your kind, and if you turn out like the others, well I'll never give another interview to anybody again. Ever."

I had no real choice. To abide by his wishes would be to relinquish all the fame and glory a published exclusive interview with George Harrison in a major magazine would bring, but I gave them my word, It was quite a responsibility: less than a year after my first journalistic effort, I was to bring the Beatles' message to the world. Or at least to the readers of my school paper.

So what's up

George took a swig of his carrot juice and leaned forward. Preston smiled.

"It's finally happened. I mean, five years after the formal breakup, we are coming back together."

Hearing that news was one thing. Being the first outside of those involved to hear it caused my heart to skip. George went on to relate how all four Beatles had thought it would be nice to reunite temporarily before their planned gala closed-circuit TV show to commemorate Sgt. Pepper's tenth birthday in 1977. He said the five—the Beatles and Preston—were rehearsing in New York in preparation for a spring mini-tour.

"Before the Beatles broke up, we all wanted to hit the road again but the argument was how to go about it. John wanted to hit the large halls. Paul wanted to book an assumed name and show up as the Beatles—, by the time the press would hear about the show would be over. Richie and me didn't care, as long as we got an audience. We were leaning toward Paul. He was full of shit about nearly everything else so me and Ringo couldn't go with Paul there if we were on John's side with business stuff. That's partly why we all split."

I asked Billy if, after two near-consecutive Beatles-related tours, he was losing his own creative touch. "Nothing from nothing leaves nothing," he shot back.

George fell silent and he asked the waiter for another carrot juice, his fourth. I suggested that he ease up if he was going to drive. Ha ha ha, George. He glares back at me and starts up again.

"*I don't really know why people won't let me have my religion. I mean, they want the music without the mantra and they're both equal parts of me. So I can't compromise. It would be easier for you to compromise.*"

Now, now, don't get angry. I'm your loyal fan. He tells me I can ask him one more thing and then he will split. So, will there be another Beatles album? George says, "Yeah, we get it when we were all drunk up in the Catskills. We thought of calling it 'Band on the Rum' but Ringo suggested 'Old 10 Eyes is Back.'"

Ten eyes? Was this a reference to Billy? "No, it's John. He wears glasses." Ha ha ha George. Something tells me our heroes have lost their subtlety.

George stood suddenly, putting on his OM and WIN buttons, shocked the crease out of his paisley jacket, and began chanting a soft mantra. I asked Preston what he thought of the project.

"That's the way God planned it," he said, leaving the check. I paid it, then went outside and panhandled for the bus fare home.

The Montgomery College Spur
March 31, 1975

Tactlessness/2

———

August, 12, 1975: Amsterdam

WHY DID YOU WEAR THESE pants, right here and right now? You got them from at a surplus store in Bethesda because they were cool, but never had the stones to wear them anywhere but at a party. You liked the fact they were on sale and the right size as there aren't a lot of 30-waist, 28-inseams available. And you're not a skillful enough seamster to shorten them to the right length.

They were unlike any jeans you'd ever seen, anywhere. Each leg had six-inch-high horizontal stripes in alternating colors: red, yellow, bright blue and orange. They really made an impression. So wearing them on the way to buy hash in a foreign city could have ended up as being a not-so-good-thing.

You are really nervous, for two reasons. Your cousin gave you the address of the dealer, sort of. She said it was three blocks from the Anne Frank house. You were to face the house and turn left, go down two blocks and turn right. After one block turn left, it was in the middle of the next block with a picture of Fidel Castro in the window.

You didn't think that you would actually score, and didn't put too much thought into what you were wearing. Imagine the surprise when Castro was right there in the window. Not Castro, actually, but Che Guevara. Close enough.

The door was opened by a guy in tie-dye and long braided hair. You were ready with the password, "Deneuve," but the guy let you in. You were told to sit and wait, next to a cheekboned Scandinavian girl who didn't acknowledge your arrival.

You never knew what to say to cute strange girls, but it wasn't your fault this time because there was a language barrier.

After about twenty minutes, the guy came back and the girl spoke.

"How long will this take?" she said, in a Boston accent.

"Not long" was the answer. You debated telling her that you were starting at Boston University next month but figured it was too late for conversation. A few minutes later an American came in, named Matt, and we did the deal. "You want to try it first?" he said. "Sure," you said, thinking you'd pay a little extra, but he chipped off a piece of your new stash. After one hit your head started swimming, and you stood up and walked out the door without saying goodbye. You were halfway down the block before realizing that Matt was still smoking a chip of your hash.

And why did you wear these pants, right here and right now?

You followed the sound of guitar music and came upon a fountain where a guy with sandy hair and a scrawny mustache was playing Neil Young's "Cowgirl in the Sand" for about thirty people. You can play this song better than him, although you weren't quite sure about the chords for "It's the woman in you that wants to play this game" part.

He finished the song with a big fat grin and to light applause. You spoke up loudly, as much a surprise to me as it must have been for him.

"Mind if I play a tune?"

"I certainly do," he said, losing the fake smile.

As I walked away he began "All Along the Watchtower." You knew this one well, and could play it and sing it way better than this guy. You had no idea what the words meant, but no one does.

You turned the corner and started shaking even though it's really hot. What if Scrawny Stache had handed over the guitar? You would have bombed. It was his audience and it was wrong to think you could win them over, especially with these pants. All anyone would remember was the pants, which you could never wear again.

You go to the hostel and change. You have the hash now and might as well go back to Brussels. A guy at the hostel said that before crossing the border you should put it in a scrunched-up paper cup on the floor. If they decide to search, you'll be clean. But what if someone comes in to collect the trash? You'll take the chance. You still have to get through the night, sleeping underneath who knows what.

You went out for a walk, in normal clothes, and passed Scrawny Stache, carrying a big blue Martin case. You looked up as he passed and he glared back. You looked down a bit ashamed, caught in a deception. If he had loaned the guitar you would have choked.

Or maybe you won after all. He didn't want to give up his audience because for all he knew you really were way better than him. You looked the part. For all he knew, these magic psychedelic pants indicated an unbelievable fingerpicking talent, and he wasn't going to give up a sure thing.

You had prevailed in the battle of the troubadours, and didn't have to play a single note.

————

November 21, 1975, Boston

In another time and place, you would have mooned over Rhonda, sat behind her in class and followed her around school until you finally got up the nerve to ask her out, at which time she would have given you a withering stare and walked away.

You didn't go to high school with Rhonda, but had the school scene played out she would have leveled you with the same disdain in her frosty eyes.

She worked in a bank. She was now doing you a favor, so ignoring her iciness was the best strategy.

"Here you are," she said, counting out the bills. "I cashed your check so you can attend your little concert."

It was a rare bright spot in this gloomy winter, a small-hall tour by Bob Dylan and a random troupe of famous and semi-famous players known as Rolling Thunder. The ticket rules were unforgiving. Shows were announced a day or so before the performance, tickets were available in one place and they only took cash. Which is how you found yourself in Shawmut Bank around the block from the Boston Music Hall, attempting to purchase a pair of tickets for next week's performance.

You banked elsewhere, at Commonwealth, because there was a branch on campus. There were no branches nearby and the line was getting longer so time was short. You stumbled into Rhonda's bank, rain-soaked and disheveled, and smiled shyly at her. She was about your age, blonde and poised, although with a bit more makeup and jewelry than the girls you knew.

"I know I don't have an account here but I really want to go to this show," you said. "Bob Dylan."

She scrunched up her nose and you almost said, "His voice takes some getting used to but his songs are really great," until determining that her displeasure was a result of your dripping water on the adjacent deposit slips.

She asked for some ID and it got worse. A Maryland license in a Boston bank to get tickets for a New York singer. This particular shot was getting longer by the minute,

She scrunched her nose again, looking away and reading something. She walked away, talked to an older lady of about forty, who had even more makeup and jewelry. The Rhonda of the future. She returned to deliver the killer line.

"I will cash your check so you can attend your little concert."

You had not disclosed that you had caught the show two weeks before in Providence. But that wasn't enough and you wanted more.

The Providence show was three hours long but you somehow missed it. Dylan appeared about halfway in but you were so wrapped up with the idea of seeing him in the flesh that the music was almost unheard. The only exception came during some of the new songs, about which you had no preconceived notions. Especially powerful was a number called "Isis," which repeated the same progression endlessly but louder and more energized each time.

Walking away from the box office, you again had two tickets and again had no idea whom to ask. There was still a chance you'd find someone in a bookstore or at a bus stop. This was not a sure thing. What was certain is that an opportunity would present itself if you only bought a single ticket.

You went around the block and walked in front of Shawmut Bank, looking in the window. You were certain Rhonda saw you as she pretended not to.

You walked around the block again, on a mission to ask her to go to the show with you. This time she saw you for sure and clearly wasn't too happy about it.

You hated what she was thinking, that was an idiot to go out into the rain and walk into a bank when they should be in class to spend money you didn't have to see a singer that no one that she knew ever liked. She resented that while she was around your age you were off chasing a musical whim while she was stuck in the bank, nine to five, with two fifteen-minute breaks and a half-hour lunch, and when she got home her parents wouldn't let her have a drink while her dad got fucked up on beer.

So in the middle of her miserable life what right did she have to judge you?

Travelogue

—

December 12, 1976, Salt Lake City

THIS IS A BETTER HOTEL room than on the rest of the trip. It has a real bedroom with a door that allows me to sit at the table and type while she sleeps. After we checked in she went in and shut that door. There could be stormy-temper weather tomorrow, but things are quiet for now. So I may as well write some of this shit down. I do need to type softly, though.

We've come to the end of this particular road. It's up for grabs, whether it ends in a cul-de-sac where we can turn around, or go over a cliff. After her little ambush tonight, wanting to go home for Christmas, it could go either way.

We saw the Bee Gees, barely making it to the show. We left Grand Junction around noon for the four-hour drive but the weather slowed us down. Once we got to Salt Lake it was past dark and we got lost a few times before finding the concert hall, and didn't get time to eat anything beforehand.

So we were both a bit grumpy. We were tired, hungry and in unfamiliar surroundings. When the band hit the stage, we were expected to have a good time then and there, which didn't happen because I was too focused on what was next, after the show ended.

The Bee Gees are a huge deal for me but interest her only peripherally. If not for my devotion she would not have driven around the west for ten days with a Bee Gees show as the eventual destination. If not for my devotion, it would probably not occur to Her to ever attend one, even if it was across the street.

Now that the ride is over, we're completely disconnected. She wants to head east to spend Christmas with her parents, which is exactly the wrong direction for me.

The show was packed, in a huge auditorium filled to the edges with people in short haircuts and mid-thigh dresses. No one was smoking. She clapped after every song but looked bored. I could tell she wanted to leave but wasn't going to miss "Lonely Days." It wouldn't have made any real difference if I'd offered to leave since whatever is going to happen will happen anyway. The inevitability of a spat increased my selfishness and a desire to keep Her here until the very last note.

I came out here without much of a plan, aside from the desire to find somewhere to complete my last semester of college in proximity to where she will be, a desolate outpost on the Navajo reservation where she will work as a nurse.

She picked me up in Gallup two weeks ago and we did the big Western loop: Grand Canyon. Phoenix. Tucson. Silver City. Socorro. Albuquerque. Santa Fe. I ran out of cash pretty quickly and sold Her my camera for fifty dollars, and she gave most of the cash back for gas. Seeing the Bee Gees was a goal, something I wasn't sure she wanted to do in the first place. I wasn't going to ask if she wanted to skip the concert because I feared the answer. She certainly didn't share my obligation to use the free tickets.

But on the way into Salt Lake, right before the show, She announced the intention to head home for Christmas and then return in January to start the job. I was welcome to drive back to DC with her, which I don't want to do. I have no money saved and if I return home I won't be able to afford to come back. I'd rather forge ahead than admit defeat, even if I go broke again.

I should write a few paragraphs here about how much I needed this to work, how it is a bad idea to go back and how much I want Her to stay and leave it around for her to read. Not going to try that because I'm not very good at manipulation and it would certainly backfire. And because it would be too indirect, even for me.

Truth is, I would never leave her on my own. She is driving and I don't want to be out in the cold right now. If She really wants to go back East I'm not going to try to stop her, but I'm not going back either.

If we drove around for another two weeks it wouldn't be good for anybody. We do, after all, have our whole lives ahead of us. Unless we kill each other.

Territory

AFTER SHE DROPPED ME OFF in Denver I hitchhiked around the west and ended up in Albuquerque, where Boston's massive crowds and fatty pastrami sandwiches were replaced by a sparse population, bright lights and all-you-can-eat-synthetic Mexican food. Discouragement morphed into opportunity. In Boston it took a month for the *Globe* to send me a letter declining to publish my short record review. In Albuquerque I just walked into the *Journal* newsroom, made my pitch, and walked out with an assignment.

It seemed too good to be true. And it was. The arts editor said they needed someone to interview and review Fleetwood Mac in advance of their March 7 *Rumours* tour, six weeks away. He gave me the assignment "depending on how you do on these stories." Just after another reporter stood up, exhaled, and left the newsroom.

The arts editor must have gotten a talking-to, because after that the reporter—Denise— had first pick of all the assignments. I got her rejects, which included Electric Light Orchestra, Jose Feliciano and a double bill of Willie Nelson and Dolly Parton. I knew little about either one, aside from a two-years-ago classmate who said that Dolly was the real deal despite her artificial look.

Bob, whom I met on the bus to Albuquerque, said Willie Nelson was great. Since he and Pam had put me up for a week when I first got to town there was a way to return the favor by giving him my plus-one ticket.

I left Bob in our seats and started exploring. At the stage I ran into Bill, who worked at the music store on Central. Wild West Music, they called it. I told Bill I was covering the show for the *Journal*, and he asked if I wanted to come backstage and meet Willie.

"I wouldn't know what to say to him," I said. "I can't name a song that he's done."

"Come on back, he's a great guy" was Bill's response. He opened the gate at stage right.

I walked through the backstage to see Willie, wearing jeans, a plaid shirt and blue track shoes. Bill introduced us.

"I don't know much about your music but I look forward to the show," I said.

"Thanks," Willie said, scowling and turning away.

"You insulted him," Bill said.

"I warned you," I said.

Bill asked me if I wanted to meet Dolly. I declined. She had her back to us; all I could see was a mound of bright blonde hair and a rhinestoned back. I was far outside of her world, and would certainly insult her more than I did with Willie.

I walked back to my seat as the lights went down and began taking notes. From my review:

Dolly Parton began her upbeat show with the soul classic "Higher and Higher," leading directly into "Silver Threads and Golden Needles," which has become a country-rock standard. Regardless of any preconceived notions concerning country music, bleached wigs and rhinestone pantsuits, it is impossible to dislike Dolly Parton.

Her clear voice has the plaintive quality exclusive to country music and her lively personality immediately puts any audience at ease. She often lets loose with a delightful, little-girl laugh (at the most inappropriate times). Even though her physical appearance smacks of artificiality, she gives the impression of being very real and warm. Her newer music will undoubtedly gain her wider appeal, but she seems to have reached that point as a result of a natural progression rather than commercial compromise.

I really dug her, and rethought Bill's invitation to meet because now I'd have something to say. I didn't know what, but I could have at least gushed a bit.

Nelson was less involved or involving, turning enjoyment into assignment. I was in a place where I didn't write unfavorable things about anybody, especially when I didn't really get their music.

Back to the review:

Willie Nelson's subdued stage presence was pale in comparison to Dolly but he was no less skilled in giving the audience what they came for. Nelson was once a key member of the Nashville music establishment until he left and essentially "let his hair down." Now, Nelson appears in jeans, plaids and blue track shoes.

His set consisted of well-paced songs with almost no break in between—and was liberally spiced with humor. He did a tongue-in-cheek medley of "Up Against the Wall, Redneck Mother" and "Okie From Muskogee." "Red Headed Stranger" told the tale of a man who shot a beautiful woman who was trying to steal his horse (an entirely "justifiable" killing). Nelson had an adept band that featured his sister, Bobbie, on keyboards—but he did his own lead playing on an ancient Martin guitar. He treated the audience to a six-song encore—and then signed autographs and traded gifts with fans until the auditorium's midnight curfew had to be enforced.

Which is where I came in. Willie stood at the edge of the stage, in his jeans, plaid shirt, blue track shoes, a bandana and a huge diver's watch, signing pieces of paper and record albums that were thrust his way. But one guy took it to another realm.

"Hey Willie, want to trade bandanas?" Willie said OK. They made the trade and the guy walked away grinning.

"Hey Willie," I said. "Want to trade watches?"
Willie scowled and walked away.

————

January 1978

Sue or Sally or Sunny somebody called me at work on Monday morning and said that Jackson Browne's management didn't want me to review his Albuquerque show two days later. It was the beginning of the tour and there were likely to be some rough spots, they said.

"Well, that's disappointing," I said. "I was looking forward to the show."

Which was something of an understatement. I knew that it was the tour's first show, a fact I used to successfully pitch it as a concert review for the inside back page of *Rolling Stone*. Something aligned because they gave me the assignment, on spec of course. They were taking a chance on me, and I was not sure I'd be able to pull it off.

I had plans to take Thursday and Friday off to write the piece, which was due the following Monday, a week from now. It was a carefully choreographed plan that had gone to shit.

She had an alternative.

"I talked to Chet," she said, referring to my editor. "He's agreed that we can fly you to El Paso for Friday's show or to Dallas on Saturday, which would be better for us because El Paso might still be a little rough." Dallas would be better for me, I said, as El Paso seemed less interesting.

"Don't worry," she said. "We'll get you on an early plane out on Sunday and you'll be back in plenty of time to meet your deadline." Apparently Chet had shared a lot with her about me and they both were overestimating my abilities. But I was back on track and I didn't care.

I got to Albuquerque on Wednesday, intending to stay with Bob and Pam. Which was now Pam, since Bob had moved back to New Jersey. I dropped off my stuff and went to the show, which was in the same small hall where I'd seen Dolly Parton and Willie Nelson a year earlier. And I sat in more or less the same seat, along the side in the front row about halfway back.

I saw Sally or Sue's point about rough spots, although if I were reviewing the show I would have given them a pass. I took notes but didn't pay all that much attention since I was honor-bound to not review this particular show. It was background that would presumably help me write the real review on Sunday.

I had brought my typewriter and slammed out a few paragraphs but couldn't get anywhere. I can't ever write anything unless the deadline is in my face. That trait would make me a better journalist, one of my teachers said, but it made the whole process pretty scary. I wasn't sure I'd be able to finish a polished review and submit it by Sunday night, but that was part of the thrill.

On Saturday I dropped my car at the airport, paid the three-dollar parking fee and headed off to Dallas. I had a small bag, a notebook, a clunky cassette recorder and a film can full of pot rolled up inside of a pair of socks.

Walking out of the gate I saw two dark-haired women, one straight-hared and the other curly, holding a sign that said ROLLING STONE.

I walked up to the curly-haired one and nodded. "I'm Sue," she said. "This is Sally." So maybe I wasn't hearing double. We were going to a hotel in downtown Dallas and have lunch before they took me to Fort Worth and my own hotel, so I could wash up before the show.

I didn't have all of Browne's albums, only the first one and the most recent, *Running on Empty*. There was a song I'd heard on the radio that I wondered about.

"What's the name of the song where he's singing about his pregnant wife?" I ask. "Ready or Not," snapped Sally. Or Sue. "Don't ever mention that song to him." Added the other one, "It was about Phyllis."

His wife, who had committed suicide nearly two years before.

At that time I wasn't recalling the nesting lyrics from "Ready or Not"; the lyrics running through my brain came from the latest album, Browne's version of "Cocaine":

"You take Sally, I'll take Sue. There ain't no difference between the two."

We drove to Fort Worth and Sally/Sue dropped me off at my hotel, gave me my pass and told me to get to the hall, a few blocks down the street, by around seven p.m. I took a nap, a shower and rolled a joint that I smoked halfway down in the bathroom with the fan on. This was Texas, after all.

The assigned seat wasn't great, off to the side and about halfway up, but the pass allowed me to walk around. Karla Bonoff played and I didn't pay much attention since I'd seen her three days ago in Albuquerque, and she wasn't all that interesting.

Browne started up with "The Fuse," followed by "Take It Easy," as he did in Albuquerque. I stood about halfway back off to the left side. I would get closer later, right now I was just taking in the atmosphere and looking for the opportunity to smoke the other half of that joint.

The urge struck when he began "Here Comes Those Tears Again." I moved to the side and turned my head, ready to light up.

"Hey, Rolling Stone." A female voice, someone who'd seen my pass.

"Hi," I said, turning to see a tall blonde in a plaid shirt and studded blue jeans.

"Want to share?"

"Sure." I passed the joint over to her, unlit. She put her hand on mine as I lit the joint, took a long draw and handed it back to me. I took my turn as my mind tried to figure out how I'd fit a one-nighter in between covering the concert and writing the review.

Which turned out to not be an issue. I handed the joint back to her but someone grabbed my arm. Someone else grabbed hers. "Come with us," they said.

We were led through a metal door where there were quite a few long-haired people looking really unhappy. I sat down. My new girlfriend was right behind me telling me to keep my mouth shut.

My life had pretty much ended. I get arrested in Texas with drugs and no money. Three people would be really pissed at me, my boss, my *Rolling Stone* editor and my father, who would be the most fearsome. There was no way I'd make it back to Espanola by Monday, which would jeopardize my job. And how was I going to write the review if I'm in jail and only saw four songs from the concert? Maybe I can cobble something together from the Albuquerque show. Or maybe my career was over before it even started.

A guy in a stiff blue shirt and black jeans came up to me and flashed a badge.

"Here's what's going to happen," he said. "We are going to search you and if we find any more drugs, we will take you to jail. If you voluntarily give up what you are carrying, we won't take you in."

I hesitated. How can I trust you? And do I really want to give up the possibility of getting high for the rest of the weekend? Time for sacrifice. I dug out the film can and handed it over. He patted me down and told me to get the fuck out of there.

Back outside Browne was finishing "Cocaine." I didn't know what I'd missed so this was going to be tricky if I was going to provide a play-by-play. Or maybe not, maybe I don't need to write down the names of every song.

I saw my almost-sweetie a few feet to the side talking to a guy who was lighting a joint. Our eyes met and she stage-mouthed "Don't you dare."

I was falling behind and began taking notes. My mind wasn't on the music, no surprise, but I couldn't focus on what I was supposed to talk about.

Browne picked up the pace and finished off with "The Load-Out," a song about playing to a large enthusiastic audience which he was now playing to large enthusiastic audience. Maybe I could put that in the review. Maybe this will work after all.

I spent the last few songs up front to the side where Sally/Sue spotted me and invited me backstage for food and beer. "But," she added, "don't talk to Jackson."

I sat in a corner of the room attempting to strike up a conversation with his band members. They were polite but kept looking over my shoulder at anyone else who walked into the room who might be more interesting.

The party broke up and Sally/Sue offered me a ride back to the hotel, but I wanted to walk back. They told me they wouldn't be able to drive me back to the airport the next day, and gave me twenty-five dollars for a cab.

I went back to the room and couldn't sleep because I was too jumpy and didn't have any pot to smoke. I wrote down a few things and got up early, taking a four-dollar bus and using the rest for breakfast in Fort Worth and lunch in Albuquerque.

The plane landed around ten thirty, gaining an hour when it was most needed. I got my car, grabbed a burger at the Frontier before heading over to Pam's. She let me into a vacant apartment next door, telling me to clean up afterward.

The only furniture in the large studio was a table and chair, which was perfect. I brought in my typewriter, a pack of paper, glue and scissors, and started typing from my notes.

An hour later I'd typed five not particularly compelling pages, gluing them together in sequence to make a one-yard-long scroll. I red-penciled it twice, rearranging the paragraphs by cutting them out and pasting them into a new location. I'd write a new paragraph, slipping it in where it belonged.

It was a struggle because I had lots of notes but no keen or unique observations. I had re-read concert reviews from the last few issues of *Rolling Stone*, which were always on the inside back page and written in an I-know-better-than-you voice.

I described the circling nature of "The Load Out," a sharp observation that gave me hope. I didn't see that it was necessary to name any band members, except guitarist Danny Kortchmar, comparing his interaction with Browne to that of David Bowie and Mick Ronson. Like Ronson, Kortchmar had the same fluid nature and smooth motion, along with a long, pointed nose. Maybe I should leave that part out.

One more hour and it was shaping up, so I retyped it onto four new sheets—it was getting shorter—and pasted them together, and started the cut/paste/write/paste process again.

Ninety minutes later, it was ready to go. I walked across the street to Davy's, a dirty diner that used to be a Denny's but lost its franchise. I stood at a pay phone just inside the door and read the piece to an operator who promised me that it would be delivered as a mailgram to *Rolling Stone* in New York the next day.

I left the final piece in the phone booth as I'd read it in print soon enough. I drove back to Espanola, heated up the bedroom and fell asleep, not even noticing that I hadn't smoked any pot all day and all I had to drink was coffee and a beer.

Back home, no one at paid any attention or asked about my trip. I worked for three days, covering a school-board meeting and writing a feature story about a local artist. On Thursday I got a letter from Chet at *Rolling Stone*: *Sorry, the Sex Pistols chose this week to break up so we're not going to run your piece. Send me a bill for your mailgram and any other expenses. I liked reading it, by the way.*

I decided to not send the bill because I had failed, until I added up all the expenses and it came to about sixty dollars. More than half of one week's salary. I'm not giving that up.

Leading up to the show I'd listened to Browne a lot, mostly from a tape made from a two-hour assortment played by an Albuquerque radio station. Once home, I didn't feel the urge to hear him again for a long while. When the tape broke I didn't care that much, as I'd heard the songs so many times that they were burned into my brain. I could evoke them any time I wanted.

I always over-prepare when given an assignment, going to the library and bookstore to find all available information about the subject and acquiring all of their records. I read the material while listening to their music, and after a few days I'm more or less ready to go. I follow this path whether I am intimately familiar with someone's art and life, or know little or nothing at all. I know how a naive or uninformed point of view can make people stop reading a story in the middle of a sentence.

I knew something about Browne on the surface and he wasn't my favorite; at that time I gravitated toward Fleetwood Mac and the Kinks. This was a project, an assignment, an opportunity to get into *Rolling Stone*. Which sank the whole thing. I wrote it as if it were a term paper instead of something that originated from a beating heart or a facile mind.

Trickster

——

Once upon a time, depending on your preferences, you would go to a concert where you would want either to sleep with a performer or be like them. For most people, this meant learning how to play the guitar, dress outrageously or fake a British accent. This wasn't enough for some people, who parlayed a slight resemblance to a celebrity into a full-blown impersonation, using the similarity to score gifts and chicks. Aside from a resemblance, these perpetrators required a willingness to lie consistently and play charades for real.

Modern tricksters need to find a different way to fulfill their fraudulent impulses. If someone were to today claim they were the guitar player in Nazareth, people would go straight to their phones for a comparison shot. If that person were to claim he was born and raised in Carlsbad, New Mexico, a quick trip to Wikipedia determines he was born in Spain. Today, such trickery requires a certain amount of planning and technical skill. Instead of rock stars, it is more profitable to pose as a Nigerian prince.

January 10, 1979, Carlsbad, NM

Just when it seems this town is too dull for words something interesting happens.

I went to the Ramada Inn because Paula the waitress called me at the paper and said there was someone that I needed to meet. I would have asked more questions, or any questions at all, but I had no plans for the week, or the month even, aside from finishing writing the annual special community promotion section, known for some reason as the "Progress" edition, of the local daily, the *Current-Argus*.

Paula turns out to be tall and nice-looking and talks with a drawl, deliberately mangling grammar. She is hiding her intelligence and playing the part of a waitress until she finds something better. But I'm guessing. Maybe she really is a little dim.

I get there and she tells me that Manny Charlton is in town. Who, right? It's her turn to think that I'm stupid. He's the guitar player for Nazareth, she says. Aren't they from England or somewhere, I ask. Yeah, but he grew up here, she says. I never knew that, but why would I? I've only lived here a few months, and never liked Nazareth enough to learn their names.

She gets me a beer and a few minutes later a skinny guy with long stringy hair walks in and looks around. Paula waves and he sits down. So does she. End of shift.

He acted indifferently, or more so than he had a right to. She introduced us. We shook hands and he looked at me like I should know who he was. Which I did, now, sort of.

"You're Nazareth," I said, my nervous inability to provide a modifier like "play with" made him smile, a little.

He said that he grew up in town and was coming back to visit his parents for a few days. No, he didn't graduate from high school. Instead he went to England and met up with the other three Nazareth guys and the rest was history.

I asked him if we can talk tomorrow. He wasn't thrilled and became less so when I suggested meeting at eleven thirty. He asked Paula if she thought breakfast would be over by then. I was losing him. I pitched three thirty. He was less displeased and and agreed to meet me at the office.

Yes, he knew where it was. He had a paper route in the seventh grade and he was on the loading dock six afternoons a week. And he'll talk to me, but only if I published the piece after he'd left town, the day after next.

Which is fine with me. I don't know anything about Nazareth. I never heard the words "Manny Charlton" before tonight. But I have all day tomorrow to do my research and figure out some intelligent questions. More for Manny than my boss or the readers, at this point. And it crosses my mind more than once tonight that an interview with a rock star about his small-town childhood might get published in the real world.

More to the point, after months of interviewing farmers, rednecks and potash miners, I'm not going to allow an actual musician to escape.

————

January 11

The guy's a fake. He didn't even show up for the interview, so I couldn't nail him on it. I visualized him walking in at three thirty and pretending to be Manny when I whipped out evidence of his true identity. But I guess you can't run a scam like this for very long without knowing when people start to get wise.

I went to sleep all excited about writing a cool small-town boy-makes-good, birth-of-a-rock-star piece for *Rolling Stone* or somewhere. Waking up, I wasn't completely convinced it was real. And it wasn't.

This morning I came in to work all excited and told The Boss about what happened last night, expecting he'd think it was as cool as I did. He didn't. If he's really Manny, it might be something for the society page, he said, and if he wasn't there is no story. I didn't try to convince him. Poor guy is barely forty and he's stuck editing a small paper in a narrow-minded town. He doesn't know that he's miserable.

Other than that, the day began optimistically. I called the LA office for A&M Records but they were an hour behind and all I could get was the secretary. I left a message: I worked for a newspaper in southern New Mexico, the same town where Manny Charlton grew up and was now visiting.

I know how the publicity game works. Record companies are eager for coverage outside of the music press, which gives the artist access to a new audience. I had also learned about the trade-offs, in which a company would grant access to an A-list artist in exchange for coverage of a lesser one. I guessed that a hometown-boy-makes-good piece might buy me a front-row seat for Peter Frampton or Nils Lofgren or someone cool down the line.

At noon I went into the town's only record store and flipped through the Ns, wanting to compare the Manny I met with the one on the album jacket just to make sure. No success there; the two albums in stock had drawings on the front and fuzzy pictures that could have been anyone. Although the large mustache and the fuzzy hair made the whole thing possible.

I still didn't know anything either way. I feared that "Manny" would turn out to not be Manny and I'd have to go back to covering the city council and the school board.

The guy at the register, Gary, grew up in Carlsbad and had a way better mustache than Manny, either real or fake. He asked me if I was "falling for that line." When I asked what he meant, he threw me a "don't be stupid" look. He talked about how "Manny" had come into the store the day before with Paula, showing off the albums. The pictures weren't at all conclusive. Gary said that Paula fell for it, but he thought I'd be smarter.

Gary told me that Paula wasn't the only dumb one, that "Manny" wasn't really paying attention, otherwise he would have recognized him. They were in the same eighth-grade class. I pointed out that Gary probably looked a bit differently then too. Without the mustache. He glared at me again.

Gary said that "Manny" was really Arlo Nestor (the name has been changed for my own protection), a thief and a liar in junior high who obviously hadn't changed much.

Back at the office, there were three messages to call A&M records. Unlike when I call requesting tickets or interviews the call went through right away. The guy who took the call, Bob, sounded pretty important and said the record company had been looking for Fake Manny for a while. He was traveling all over pretending to be the guitarist, usually targeting women and even appearing on the radio a few times in character. He'd also managed to bill hotel rooms and meals to the record company.

The real Manny, Bob said, was pretty pissed about this and wanted it to stop. Bob said he's a record-company guy and not a detective, that Nazareth was an important band, and wanted them to be happy. I knew they had been at it a while and were probably miffed about being surpassed by that whipper-snapper-label mate Peter Frampton a few years back. If I could help out, the label would fly me to a nearby show and I could meet them backstage. I didn't let on that I would rather meet Peter Frampton.

Bob said they didn't even know who the fake Manny was, so I clued him in them in to Arlo Nestor and told him that he was scheduled to come into the office. Bob got really excited, saying that I needed to call the police and have him arrested. I don't have a great relationship with the Carlsbad cops, so I looked up the number and passed it to Bob, who said he'd call them right away.

He called me back ten minutes later saying the cops weren't going to do anything, and that I should still attempt to detain him when he showed up. I had no idea how I could possibly do that, I didn't think Bob was really thinking clearly about this. I said I'd try but guessed that it wouldn't be an issue because Fake Manny probably wouldn't show. Which he didn't.

The next idea was to track down Paula but when I went to the Ramada they told me she had called in sick. It occurred to me to look in the phone book where I found a listing for Arlo Nestor Sr., guessing that he was Fake Manny's dad.

He was getting out of the car when I pulled up. I nearly said I was a friend of Arlo's from school and that I'd heard he was in town but telling lies never works for me. So I told him I was from the *Current-Argus* and was trying to do a story about Arlo.

Arlo Sr. wasn't fooled by that. What has he done now, he asked. Usually he doesn't pull any shit around here because people know him.

I asked if he'd seen Arlo this time. He told me it was none of my business and went inside the house.

I wasted the day but it really didn't matter. I have most of the Progress edition written and there were no daily assignments aside from The Boss telling me that I needed to get started on that series about the local potash industry.

He hasn't said much about the whole Manny thing specifically since knocking down the idea this morning, except in passing. He didn't expect me to work here long, he said, but while I was here I needed to be present. OK, then. I'll try it your way.

———

January 15

I thought about Fake Manny all weekend and came in with the story pitch. The Boss held his ground, but I have to give him credit for listening.

I set it up, how an aspiring delinquent leaves town to make a living impersonating a marginal rock star, committing acts of petty fraud. I would talk to his teachers and his friends as well as the record company and trace their pursuit of Fake Manny.

Do you know any of his friends or teachers, The Boss asked.

No, but I can find them, I said.

Will his father talk to you, he asked.

He didn't want to before for publication but I can convince him, I answered. This part was a lie. The old guy would not budge.

Has the record company sworn out a complaint or any charges, he asked.

Not that I know about, they don't want the attention I answered.

I don't see this as a story, he said. I don't think our readers care.

I stifled the urge to argue it further. I got up without a word but he had the last one, saying that I could write an op-ed about the experience if I wanted, since the standards for columns aren't the same and I can include my opinions.

"I'd like you to write columns," he said. "I think you'd be really good at it."

Sure, but if I could sell the piece to *Rolling Stone* or even the *Albuquerque Journal* I'd get way more readers and may even end up on microfilm in a library somewhere. A column on the back page of the local paper in the middle of January isn't going to reach more than a few hundred people.

His parting shot sealed the article's fate, with instructions to make the column more about me than about Fake Manny.

So here goes.

Rock and Roll Imposter

As a precocious 12-year-old, I had none of the same uncertainties as my classmates. I already knew it I was going to be in my later years. I was going to be someone that all my classmates would brag about having grown up with. I was going to be a hit at parties as well as at class reunions.

I was going to be a rock star.

The uncertainties set in a bit later, after I found out a mastery of skills as well as the patience to rehearse. Perseverance was needed to accomplish what I stated as goals; being cute wasn't enough.

There are no statistics as to how many had similar ambitions but judging by the small amount of rock stars today quite a few people went through the same metamorphosis as I did, not finding the right combination of talent, perseverance and luck and finding a life that didn't involve fame or fortune.

This week I met someone who found a compromise, achieving a sort of rock-star status without possessing any of the aforementioned qualities. This former Carlsbad man has apparently made a career for impersonating a guitarist in the Scottish rock band to whom he bears a slight resemblance, reaping some of the benefits of stardom.

Since the group is not that well-known (certainly not in this area) there are not very many people who would dispute the word of such an enthusiastic and personable character. Most people believe he is who he says because they've never heard of them.

(Personally, if I were going to say I was a rock star I'd pretend to be a member of KISS. No one would ever know for sure.)

What does he stand to gain by this little charade? An impersonator's lot is not a happy or stable one, as he must get out of each town before the ruse is discovered. What he does get is admiration and adulation; many people have never seen a real live rock star in the flesh. That, along with the abundance of women who are eager to hang out with someone who has made a record.

Rock stars are the only people to have groupies. There are even some women who go nuts over writers, or at least that's what I hear. But for some reason the average rock star has his own aphrodisiac qualities.

Representatives of the group's record company and management were nearly violent when discussing the impersonator. One lady from New York gave me strict instructions to call Carlsbad police and have the impostor arrested immediately. These people tried frantically to swear out a warrant for the man's arrest but his alleged crimes—charging small bills and making promises on behalf of the band—were not serious enough to warrant extradition.

In the meantime, the impostor rode up to Roswell, where he appeared on a radio show and signed autographs at a local record store. You have to admire his nerve.

Now I can't totally condone this charade. The guy is taking advantage of people's better nature, and a lot of them will treasure these autographs along with their family Bible.

The Kinks, the group that has been singing rock as well as singing about it for fifteen years, tell the story of someone who lives his life in a rock 'n' roll fantasy: when he feels down, he puts some rock 'n' roll on and it makes him feel all right, and when he feels the world is closing in, he turns his stereo way up high. Music has been performing the same function for centuries but the feelings into the new media age have never been so universal.

The impersonator, again, is just trying to live the dream that most of us gave up sometime ago. He has played this game for several years and his father, a respected Carlsbad citizen, told me that his son comes to town early each year for his birthday and to say hello to folks.

So next year someone should come up to you in a record store and say he's a member of the band that you never heard of, you don't have to let on that you know he's a fake. Just ask for his autograph and let him live his rock 'n' roll fantasy.

Carlsbad-Current Argus, January 29, 1979

———

February 18
What a colossal fucking waste of time today was.

After "Manny" escaped last month, I called Bob at A&M, expecting that he'd be pissed. But he acted happy and generous, offering to send me copies of the new Nazareth album. I told him that I didn't have a record player, true enough, but didn't let on that I'd switched to cassettes. If he sent me something, I'd have to pretend I liked it.

After Fake Manny left town and my disclosure of his true identity, Bob called to see if I wanted to see Nazareth in Dallas on March 3. Sure, I said, but I have no way to get there. He then missed his cue, the part where he was supposed to offer to fly me in. I recovered quickly, asking for tickets to see The Tubes, who had a scheduled Albuquerque show. I had already seen them twice, and their craziness was exactly what I needed.

Bob said that two tickets would be waiting at the door.

I got up early, drove the three hundred miles to the University of New Mexico, going directly to the student union. Maybe I could find someone who'd like the extra ticket and I could stay at her house later. There was a poster for the concert with big red letters, CANCELLED, written on its front. Since I don't live in Albuquerque, I never heard. And Bob didn't think to call me with the news.

What next? I went down a list of all the people and places I knew in town and couldn't come up with anyone I wanted to see or anything I wanted to do. I headed home, thinking I'd grab a burger someplace, but didn't stop driving until Roswell, two hundred miles away, and stopped at a Wendy's.

Arlo masked

One lesson learned today is that I should live closer to the music so I don't have to go through this again. Another is to just stay put, give this place another shot, ask to stay on and give them what they think they want from me.

I should be happy right here, change my priorities, and stop thinking I need to be at every show by someone I once liked. That is my resolution.

And it will work until the Kinks play Albuquerque, and I'll do the same thing all over again.

April 4, 2017, Port Townsend, WA

You always wondered where old Arlo ended up. Ever since he eluded your questions during his Manny Charlton pose, you wanted to ask him what he was thinking. Six years after he eluded your grasp in Carlsbad you were living in San Jose and read a story about his arrest on fraud charges. You wanted to ask how and why he assumed these identities, and why he focused on Manny Charlton. Did he deliberately choose someone less famous so the average person would believe the tale? Did he run the scam in small towns because there are more Nazareth fans in big cities who knew what Real Manny looked like? Did anyone ever ask him to play guitar? Had a woman that he'd seduced as Real Manny ever find out that he was a fake? Maybe, you thought then, you wouldn't ask that one.

Later on you wonder if he is perhaps on Facebook but that strikes out, so you do a regular search. Nothing conclusive so you take a chance on searching "Arlo Nestor custody," which pops up a Florida arrest record and a mug shot. It's the same guy. The same hollow eyes and cornered look, but no mustache. He doesn't at all resemble current pictures of Real Manny, who has apparently assumed the rotund appearance of a well-respected country squire.

There is a "contact prisoners" link, which you nearly select before realizing there is no way you are going to write this guy to get his side of the story. He'd probably turn up on your doorstep. Instead you choose to rearrange the letters of his name for appropriate protection and just write down everything you can remember. Even so there is a chance that Arlo, or whatever his name really is, will one day show up in town asking for money.

From the attached picture you don't know who he could impersonate, which is probably why he turned to a life of straight crime.

A few months later you do the same search and he is gone. Escaped? Probably just back on the street somewhere. You will never seek him out. But if he ever turns up on the streets of Port Townsend, you will ask whether his time as Manny Charlton where he was treated like a celebrity and shared the grace of good-hearted and gullible women was his finest hour.

Transition

Rearranging the Furniture

December 1983, Washington DC

YOU ARE TURNING THIRTY NEXT year and realize this whole celebrity-interview thing hasn't really worked out. Even so, there is a need to continue the original mission—to use journalism as an excuse to connect with important people, which you still crave.

An answer, or at least a solution, arrives accidentally. After meeting guitarist Nils Lofgren, whom you first met in 1969 as the leader of Grin while you were still in junior high. He mentions his new album and agrees to an interview if you can promise to get it in print.

You agree and meet in your parents' kitchen, a few miles from where Nils's folks live, and write a standard profile that captures Nils's personality well. It is especially insightful, you feel, because you have already known Nils for thirteen years and can offer a perspective missing with other writers who have just made his acquaintance.

You go down the list of tour cities and call the local papers but none are interested. You are told by *Unicorn Times*, a local arts weekly, they would run the story and would even put it on the cover, but they don't pay. It turns out you've over-estimated Nils's importance. Newspapers in Baltimore, Providence, Boston and Poughkeepsie turn down the story. Spurned in Poughkeepsie. Now that boggles the mind.

With each submission, you fine-tune the piece but it still seems stilted. You call back *Unicorn Times* and offer the piece with a condition, that its presentation will be creative. The editor, who by now needs a cover story by the next day, agrees.

A regular feature story requires a beginning, middle and an end that explain the subject's various facets, tying it all together with transitions and theme. Throughout various drafts you've fallen short with the Nils piece so you set about disassembling your work. Instead of a linear narrative you divide the story into separate topics with no direct connection to each other.

This device allows you to frame the objective material with subjective observations. You are pleased with the results but they still need the theme. You count up eleven topics and write two more about luck that tie it into an unlucky number, and "Thirteen Thoughts About Nils Lofgren" is published. This proved that a theme doesn't need to follow its own rule, as the article had only twelve "thoughts" in its narrative.

The new format is liberating, and you begin to look at each new article with a theme in mind. Over the next two years you publish three additional themed-cover stories with *Unicorn Times*, of T-Bone Burnett, Fairport Convention and the Go-Go's. You borrow the technique once more for a profile of Laurie Anderson for a similarly inclined Boston-based arts magazine called *What's New*.

After three years the grand experiment was over. The themes didn't always make a lot of sense. They bounced between the ridiculously obscure or painfully obvious. For Burnett, you choose a biblical pattern which you knew he would hate because he was then best known as the person who shepherded Bob Dylan's religious conversion. Which wasn't the whole truth.

You used the device to cover up your mistakes. For the Fairport article you interviewed two band members on a duo tour, but in the cab home you discovered the tape machine had failed to record. This began a pattern. Even today you finish interviews only to discover that you never pushed the recorder's start button.

In the cab you quickly write down everything you could remember, but it's not very much. The published piece only had a few quotes from what you remembered as a pretty good chat. You made up the rest from what you already knew.

You chose the obvious English-literature theme, peppering the headlines with references to Chaucer and Shakespeare, bridging the quotes with observations you had gleaned from a two-year obsession with the Fairport tree and all its branches.

The theme, you learned, can't be too subtle or too forced. The mental-illness connection to the Go-Go's bordered on tasteless, and the reader went away thinking you had a crush on the band. Which was exactly opposite than what you intended. You walked into the interview wanting to impress them but walked out not liking them very much. That Belinda Carlisle doesn't know how to use an apostrophe was especially deflating.

Of these five "alternative" pieces, Lofgren and Burnett were successes, Fairport and Anderson were failures.

The Go-Go's sat in the middle. Their year was one of peaks and valleys. They released a phenomenal album but lost a founding member due to ego squabbles. It also turned out they lied to you about a key occurrence, explaining guitarist Charlotte Caffey's absence on the new album to the then-little-known carpal tunnel syndrome when she was actually addicted to heroin.

After a contentious interview you placed the piece in the New Orleans and St. Petersburg papers, and actually earned some money. You disassembled the piece for the *Unicorn Times*, framing it with your own fictitious nervous breakdown and adding material that called the band's management out as jerks. Although they didn't seem to notice.

The Anderson piece was assigned, with the editor commissioning you to write a cover story about this supposedly important artist about whom you knew almost nothing. You dove into the research in the same way as a school project.

Anderson, you learn, is a fascinating character and you look forward to the interview, which is to take place in her apartment just south of Canal Street in New York City. You are also told you have all afternoon for the interview, which is also exciting as it has the potential of being a deep piece.

You arrive at the apartment early and Anderson is a little frosty. She says she has about forty-five minutes, which is a bit of a shock. You had not brought a recorder because you did not want to transcribe several hours of tape, so now you are stuck taking notes on a yellow pad. Which you embarrassingly needed to borrow from Anderson. All your research time is wasted as all your well-thought-out questions do not solicit a positive reaction or even a good quote. She knew that you didn't grok her world and she didn't want to waste her time.

You have a week off from work that is devoted solely to this project so you wall yourself into your apartment and bear down. A concept is needed but it escapes you. The album that Anderson is pushing, a five-record live set called *United States*, is hard to figure out. You have listened to it start to finish twice and were still unsure what it meant. You walk down to Columbus Avenue and Broadway and buy some more pot for the next listen, but that doesn't shed any more light.

Midway you land upon a concept, a slideshow about a cross-country trip but without any slides. You hammer it out but it still seems like a stretch. You toy with the idea of writing a linear version, but the interview material isn't strong enough.

You submit the piece and it comes out two months later, looking better in print than you expected or remembered. You resolve to not write any more conceptual pieces unless the concept makes sense.

The publication of random, fractured articles was only one result of the impulse to change. You were continuing efforts to freelance more traditional pieces with some success. You were becoming involved in the personal-computer world, which both created a new career path and allowed you to more easily polish your writing.

Prior to acquiring your first computer, articles were typed out and pasted together to form one long piece of paper, a scroll, with revisions literally cut and glued together from one part of the story to the next. You would then retype and submit the final draft, but were never able to free yourself of the chicken-scratch edits.

In this new world, you pictured the article as soft cloth and the computer a hard shoe, on which you would rub back and forth until everything shone and sang.

It paid off. You soon moved to a new town with a new job that changed your life's direction. You spent the days writing about emerging technology and the evenings further developing your point of view and extracurricular writing skills.

You learned to become more free with your writing and observations, writing how you spoke. That should have been obvious since the beginning, right? So you acquired what became a preferred writing style: direct, personal and without lots of fancy words. You often read passages aloud to make sure everything flowed.

Each section became a mini-essay, where you explained a thought in the same way as on a barstool, although in a sober, cohesive way that doesn't happen with a drink in front of you.

These stories included the first realization that you did better work when you don't care whether the person you are interviewing likes you or not. Thirty years later you haven't kicked the habit but you are at least aware of the problem.

Meeting the Beatle
You defined freelance music writing through an easy, three-step process: Select the subject. Determine a target publication, usually by its proximity to a tour stop, and extract an assignment, always on spec. Then approach the subject's management as a representative of the publication.

With the addition of the *Globe and Mail* as a client, it became a breeze. It was a national paper, and nearly everyone who tours plays in Canada, somewhere.

These days you were between jobs and attempting a full-time freelance thing, knowing it wouldn't last long because you could never put enough away for taxes. So it was just lucky that George Harrison slipped into your sights at that exact time and place.

Harrison was a big enough name that touring wasn't an issue, that putting out a new album was news enough. You called up Mary, your *Globe and Mail* editor, and pitched her the idea: "If I get a George Harrison interview, would you run it?" you asked. Her response was a predictable "Well, yeah." You gained permission to contact the record company on the paper's behalf with the interview request. You made a few calls and extracted a tentative spot on the schedule the following week.

Then it fell apart. Mary's new boss asked why a paper in Toronto was hiring a writer in San Francisco to interview someone in Los Angeles by phone. He decreed that Mary should withdraw the assignment and publish the inevitable wire-service story written by someone who had actually been in the same room with the former Beatle. Mary called on the Monday prior to the Thursday appointment, opening with "I have bad news."

"What would it take to change his mind?" you asked.

"You would have to do it in person," she said. "I'm really sorry."

By two p.m. the next day you are tearing down the 101 past San Jose, on the way to LA. You had confirmed the appointment, only to the point where it was more likely to happen than not. The PR woman, Marina, was a little put out when you called her that morning and asked to switch the phoner into an actual audience.

"We can't pin down a time," she said. "It'll be sometime between one and five." "How about I get there at 1 and wait?" you ask. She agrees.

You could have driven the whole way in one day but didn't have to arrive until the day after tomorrow. You stop at Santa Barbara, staying in a huge hotel that looked like a castle. You burrowed into the room and resumed writing out the list of questions.

Interviews conducted during your day job, writing about technology and new products, were pretty spontaneous. You'd go in with a mission, needing to find out one or two specifics, and conduct something that was close to a conversation.

This hadn't quite translated to the celebrity world, where you hadn't really changed the MO developed with Diana Rigg years before: work from a list of thirty or so questions, knowing there wouldn't be time to ask them all but you would never run out of words. This wasn't a perfect system, because while the subject was answering one question you weren't paying attention, but thinking about what should come next. Active listening wasn't required, as the tape was running and you could always pay attention during the playback.

You deliberately made Wednesday easy. It was less than ninety miles to LA where you landed another hotel following breakfast, lunch, and dinner and a trip to the beach, refining the question list throughout, all in longhand. You practice them aloud, but not in public. In the room you map out the next day's journey, the twenty miles of surface streets between Hollywood and Burbank.

You arrived early enough to spend an hour in Tower Records, eat lunch and arrive at the Warner Brothers' building just before one p.m. You recalled advice about how the best interviews are conducted when the interviewer is a bit hungry but had no idea how long you'd be waiting. They weren't going to supply sandwiches, and were paranoid about your stomach's tendency toward a spontaneous growl when you're nervous. Having your stomach argue with a Beatle wasn't an option.

Marina puts you in a small office with a lot of audio equipment. This is to be expected in a major-label record company. She watches you settle on the desk, taking out a tape recorder and a copy of Harrison's book. She tells you that personal requests are forbidden, and you were not to request that Harrison sign the book. You act like that had never crossed your mind.

There is a tape in the deck marked *Cloud Nine*, Harrison's new album that wasn't due to come out for two months. Marina said you can listen to but not to tape the album. Unlike getting the book signed, this had never occurred to you, to attempt a through-the-air recording from the posh stereo to your little cassette recorder. The fidelity would suck and you didn't want to waste the batteries.

You play it once all the way through. At first listen it sounds a lot better than his last several albums. It was livelier and had at least four out-of-the-gate great songs. Which means that the others will take hold after another few listens.

So you listen to it again, and work on your questions. You know them by heart but are still going to keep the list.

The album isn't interesting enough for a third pass and you inspect some of the other tapes in the case. Bee Gees. Robbie Robertson. You left them alone, you didn't want to lose your focus and you had no received permission to change the tape.

An hour passes. You break things up with trips to the bathroom and the vending machine. Another hour and the focus is lost. You know the questions and their sequence, more or less, but the edge is gone. The excitement of meeting a Beatle is gradually forced out by a desire for a joint and a nap.

You take another trip to the bathroom. There is a guy at the next urinal with dark hair and a colorful tweed jacket. He looks at you sideways, and you realize it is Harrison. You don't say a word and wait at the urinal until he leaves the room, even though you haven't pushed out a single drop since you got there.

At around three forty-five, Marina comes in and said George is ready. She leads you to another room, a long office. You shake hands and sit down.

The first question is always general in order to get accustomed to the setting. Politicians call it "taking temperature of the room." You ask about the timing of the new record.

I was taking a break but I still continued writing and putting songs on tape. I never really stopped doing that although I never put out a record. I had a chance to get away from it for a bit, then I felt much better about the idea of doing it, and then it was a question of finding someone I could work with. It's handy to have someone to bounce ideas off of. I really miss that part of being in a group, where you can come up with all of your own ideas, and you have other people's ideas and they all mix together and they become even a different idea. Here, the whole burden isn't on just myself. I decided it was time to make a new album, but this time I was going to make it with some other producer.

I just don't really know that many record producers. So I thought who will be good? Someone I really admire and someone who would respect me and my past and not try to turn me into something I'm not. I thought of Jeff Lynne of the Electric Light Orchestra. He'd be fun.

I'd never met him. He's a very private person, Jeff, he's one person who I don't think has done interviews or television, or anything. He's just very private. Anyway I got a message to him through Dave Edmunds that I'd like to meet him. And I met Jeff, and over period of eighteen months I got to know him and suggested that I'm going to make a record and just sounded him out. And he said he'd help, (but) he never committed himself. So last November I finally said that's it, I'm going to make a record, at least get some musicians over, and so he said OK, and we worked from January, straight through until August.

Some of the album sounded fresh but was predictable when it came to the players.

When I think of who I want to play drums on a track I think of Jim Keltner. I know Jim so well, he's such a great drummer, and at the same time Ringo, because Ringo, I don't have to tell him what I want, he'll just listen to the tune and he'll play like Ringo. So same goes for guitar solos, that should be Eric on that one. So there's a lot of my same old friends. The added influence of Jeff helping to produce worked well indeed, has a good structural sense of songs, he's a composer and a guitarist himself, a lot of similarities.

He talked about the song selection process, noting that he had recorded a cover of Bob Dylan's "Every Grain of Sand." He lit up a cigarette and asked if you minded the smoke. You did, but could suffer through it. You asked about the multitude of Beatles books and whether anything was omitted. He asked you if you wanted him to tell you something that nobody else knows. You tell him no, in a later-regretted effort to protect his privacy.

A lot of the stuff in the books are wrong. A lot of them are written out of malice, or from people with axes to grind for one reason or another. And they've perverted certain things for their own gain. Not many are actually factual and honest. There is a saying in the old house that I have, it's in Latin. Translated, it says, "Those who tell all they have to tell, tells more than they know." So you probably know more about the Beatles from reading those books than there actually was.

The Beatles phenomena was bigger than life. The reality was that we were just four people as much caught up in what was happening at that period of time as anybody else.

The Beatles always had a sense of humor, so you ask what makes him laugh.

A lot of things. I've always liked comedy, back when I was a kid I liked the Goon Show, I was a big fan of Peter Sellers, and later on I was a good friend of his. I liked Peter a lot. I loved Monty Python. I couldn't explain how much I liked it. The rut that television gets into, and people's lives—Python just blew all that away by making fun of everything. Right down to the style of television we've been watching. The result is that I got to know some of them and we made The Life of Brian *and* Time Bandits *and a couple of films with Michael Palin, so that kind of stuff makes me laugh.*

He said there were no specific plans for the future, after the record-release process winds down.

It'll be pretty much the same. My film company is jogging along; we have a lot of projects. It's the sort of company that doesn't seem to make a lot of blockbuster movies; they seem to be the sort of films that nobody else wants to make. But it still doesn't mean that they shouldn't be made. The only thing that I would like to accomplish is perfect peace in a spiritual sense to be able to consciously leave my body at will.

There is no timekeeper or reminder; the interview ends when the conversation winds down. You walk out of the building and into the car and drive several blocks before you realize that you hadn't said anything to Marina on your way out. This was an involuntary act. You had kissed up to her for weeks and she treated you like a serf. You got what you wanted, and needed, then got the fuck out of there.

You drove west without a map, knowing that you'd get to a northern-heading road with a recognizable route number sooner or later. That turns out to be 101, which is pointed directly toward the ocean. It turns into Route 1, the path up the coast to San Francisco, and you don't even have to check the map.

Traffic is light, so you pop the interview cassette into the car player, tempting fate because it's been a bit finicky. It plays fine, but the disturbing part is how the little substance is there.

You kick yourself for not being more original, or provocative. You recall the prime directive, while you were still a fan and not yet a journalist, that a member of the media can use that privilege to gain access to these people. Ultimately, you accept the poor content of the interview and congratulate yourself for the ability to stay vertical and carry on a conversation that made actual sense.

You drove to LA on 101 because you were in a hurry, the trip back is more relaxed so you decide to drive up the coast the entire way. The road veers inland and you lose sight of the ocean. It winds back eventually and it gets dark as you approach a town called Morro Bay, which you recognize because it was namechecked in a Beach Boys song. You expect some kind of aquatic open space but can't see anything from the road, so you find a clapboard motel far dingier than the two previous nights' lodging. There is a TV with HBO, where an unknown rotund comedian named Roseanne Barr prattles on in the background. You don't pay attention until she says, "People say to me, "You're not very feminine." Well, they can just suck my dick."

You listen to the Harrison tape once more and it sounds better the second time, although not great. Kind of the same reaction you've had about several George Harrison albums.

Once home you unpack, but are too wired to sit down. So you go to a bar and sit with a woman on one side and a man on the other. You realize that you have done something extraordinary and want to tell someone. "You know what I did yesterday? I met George Harrison." But you hold back. If someone came up to me in a bar saying that, you would want to know every detail but you weren't willing to risk that anyone else would react the same way.

There is no rush. The *Globe and Mail* did its big arts page on Saturday, and it was too late for this week. The next morning you transcribed the tape, still not convinced the interview was any good but knowing you accomplished something by just being there.

You spend the weekend inside writing. You outline the topics, gather the quotes but still can't find the right way to start. On Monday afternoon you sit down and it pours out.

> *George Harrison has emerged to call attention to his future but willingly discusses his past. As a Beatle he was all hair, knees and teeth, physically overshadowed by Lennon and McCartney. Today he looks heavier and healthier, his medium-length styled hair is offset by a salt-and-pepper stubble. And his warmth is overwhelming.*
>
> *"I couldn't live in a house full of of journalists where they ask me questions all the time," he said. "But there are occasions like this when I come out and say hello to people."*

After this you move around some more paragraphs, add the formatting for the *Globe and Mail,* and modem it on over.

It's published Saturday. Mary has promised to drop a few in a pouch that would get here Monday but that's not soon enough. You call Air Canada for a list of planes coming in and get to the airport around three. When the plane has discharged all of the passengers, you approach the stewardess and ask if anyone has left behind a copy of today's *Globe and Mail*. You tell her that you needed an article that was published that day. She is dazzlingly beautiful, with short, bobbed blonde hair and a plump, lovely shape. You do not tell her that you had written the article or that it was an interview with a Beatle. That would put her at an unfair advantage.

She comes back with two papers. You walk a while, sit down and read the story. Too quickly, so you read it again. Back to the car, a third time.

You don't often talk to yourself but make an exception here.

"You fucking did it.

"You fucking did it.

"You fucking did it."

So what's next? Harrison isn't on tour so there is no list of cities. Which means there are no limits or restrictions. So you make a list of cities, the best papers in each, and start making calls. After a multitude of rejections, trying unsuccessfully to place interviews with Todd Rundgren and Nils Lofgren, you are inspired by your success. It always helps if you are selling something people want.

You call a paper, ask for the arts editor, and make the pitch: "I interviewed George Harrison last week for the Toronto *Globe and Mail*, and am looking to place the piece domestically." You actually say "domestically" with a straight face.

Most say yes and provide their address. Instead, you ask for the paper's modem-formatting protocols, which involved inserting special characters to break up the paragraphs and at the end of the story. This impresses them, because they won't have to do any typing.

Every day you wake up and sell the story one more time. By the end of the week you have placed with Cleveland, St. Petersburg, St. Louis, San Diego, and San Jose. You stay away from the really big papers because they would want an exclusive, and it's just too much fun selling the piece over and over. Besides, there is a guy in LA who's doing the same thing and placed his piece in the *Washington Post* and the *San Francisco Examiner*. So it's become a competition.

Each version is just a little different, since you revise it each time. By the time you get to the *Honolulu Advertiser,* it's nearly perfect. Which is where it raises to another level. "This is really good," the editor says. "You should syndicate it." You ask where and she mentions *The New York Times* syndicate, gives you the number and that you can use her name. You reciprocate and tell her she doesn't have to pay for the piece but she laughs. "I'm not management, so I don't care if the money gets spent."

The *Times* says yes, but is not pleased that it has already appeared in so many places. It is placated when you promise to stop selling the piece and withdraw it from where it has been accepted but not published. This provides yet another new experience, calling up publications and telling them to not print your story. You hope that doesn't ever come back to bite you.

It takes about a year before you stop kicking yourself for questions not asked. The checks are slowing to a trickle. You have quit your job, moved to another town, and are engaged to be married. You are no longer compelled to interview musicians and celebrities because you have been to the mountain-top. The headliner has played; now it's time to everyone to go home and do something constructive with their lives.

The thirty minutes spent with George were insignificant in length when compared with the days and months and years and decades that followed. They are further diminished by life's occurrences; a marriage, several reloca-tions, the loss of your parents, the loss of several jobs, the loss of a wife. But they were still defining moments, and you often recall those moments in a bland Burbank office. Yes, this is not a good time, you tell yourself after a set-back or an insult, but you once met George Harrison and the person annoying you did not.

In 2008, you receive an email from an associate of filmmaker Martin Scorsese, who is making a documentary about Harrison, she says, and her research has turned up a version of your interview. She is interested in any insights you may have, but is most excited about acquiring any audio, in a quest to "find never-before-published or rare materials." George gave so many interviews there was a chance they could recover a new insight.

You would willingly surrender the tape for use in the documentary if it still existed, but it had gone missing fifteen years before. You had stored all the cassette tapes in a plastic box that was moved from place to dirtier place. You had meant to convert them all to CD but never got around to it and one day the box disappeared.

Or maybe it had already been missing for a while. You determined that had been stuffed in a bag and taken to the dump during one of your mass cleanings or tossed during periodic tantrums as you struggled to find a way toward a positive life.

Their loss wasn't such a big deal at the time, as your life had changed and then centered around the emergence of new technology and getting up at dawn to feed three ungrateful horses. The greater loss was a signed John Lennon book that went missing around the same time. You imagine that one day you will find the book and the tapes again, in antique mall or a yard sale.

Aside from the life changes, you weren't sad to see the tapes go because they represented your failures. After transcription, usually on the same day as the interview, you never listened to them again. Your obvious verbal clumsiness and inability to carry on a conversation produced humiliating results. Over the years you had become a fair writer but still had trouble articulating cogent thoughts, whether it be a social event or an interview with a celebrity.

So the lost tapes become just another minor regret, not because of their significance but because they are not recoverable and it accomplishes nothing to wish otherwise. This is how you have lived your life: the loss of an object means little if all your appendages are still intact. During the more self-aware moments you recognize this as rationalization.

As you prepare material for a collection of interviews, the loss of the tapes two decades ago hits hard. You then conclude that it would not matter whether Scorsese or anyone would listen to or broadcast these tapes, and would even share your awkward interactions with Diana Rigg and the Bee Gees.

While there are many versions of the event in print, what really happened and how it felt now resides in your imagination, and in the ether.

Technology

——

AFTER THE GEORGE HARRISON ADVENTURE there was a sense that I'd reached a sort of pinnacle and needed to re-evaluate my priorities. Whomever I interviewed next would pale in comparison, so it had to be someone big or no one at all. I chose the latter, turning my full attention to technology journalism.

I had been one of the first people on my block to acquire an IBM PC in 1983. In March 1984 I took a week off from work for two freelance pieces, a personality profile for the *Washington Post* and a game review for the then-emerging *PC Magazine*. Weeks later the checks arrived, $75 from the *Post* and $300 from *PC*. Eager for new friends and more money I attended a workshop at *PC*'s headquarters for freelancers, which developed into an interview and job offer. I moved to New York City in August, with the hope of learning as much as possible about the new machines.

At that point, many computer journalists fell into one of two categories: Geeks who did not know how to write for a general audience and writers with only a superficial knowledge of computers. I fell into the second category. In the beginning, manufacturers would visit the magazine to introduce something like a tape backup system and needed to explain exactly what tape backup was.

Outside of the rare person who was dead-set to show he knew more than I did, it was an interesting, educational ride. The computer press was then hiring many writers with no tech experience, as it was easier to teach a writer how to be a geek than teaching a geek how to write.

One valuable skill was the ability to pursue and question celebrities, or people who thought themselves more significant than they actually were. They were forgiven, because they all believed they were doing great things. There were new ideas every day, and it was impossible to predict which ones would take off.

The playing field was different but the games were the same. Instead of pursuing people like The Beach Boys, Richard Thompson or George Harrison I was covering future famous people Bill Gates, Steve Jobs, Steve Ballmer and Michael Dell. As well as dozens now lost to history.

A month into the job I began hearing about the Computer Dealer's Exposition, COMDEX, a twice-yearly trade show that was the forum for new product introductions. I wasn't sure if I would be sent to cover the show, November in Las Vegas, but was given a list of companies to call about their products. This was six weeks before the show so plans were not in place, so I had to write in generalities. There was also the probability that many of the products would never make it to the market, but that wasn't a factor. If someone told us about a product we'd write it down and go to press.

I called about thirty companies, none of which I'd ever heard of. There was a lot of money behind these companies and they all hired PR agencies to field calls from the press. These agencies were staffed by young-sounding women, which immediately kicked me into flirt mode. They were smart and engaging, which led me to believe they must be attractive.

One PR person in particular was especially fun. After finishing the story about her company I found excuses to call her every week or so, when we determined we'd both be at COMDEX and should meet for a drink. I didn't know Las Vegas at all, so she suggested that we meet at 6 p.m. Friday in the lobby of the Sahara Hotel. I asked how I would recognize her. She said the was about 5'4," 180 pounds with frizzy red hair and would be wearing a muumuu.

Ummm, yeah.

At COMDEX I hit several nightly parties and drank to oblivion at the behest of a supervisor who was showing me the ropes. I was thirty years old and had never been to an open-bar party, and didn't waste any time catching up. After the mist cleared I realized these parties were held for a reason, to promote products. Which were pretty boring, most of the time. I'd meet someone at a party and strike up a conversation. I wouldn't give them a thought until the next year and the next party, where we'd pick up where we left off. Pretty soon I mastered the ability to remember who people were from one year to the next, saving some detail that made me look like I cared.

At the exact time I was supposed to meet her I was sitting at a table in the Las Vegas Country Club in the middle of a huge Microsoft party. Open bar. Food. New people. I made the decision to stay put. That evening there was a message at the hotel, "sorry I missed you." I didn't respond, nor did either of us follow up after the show.

Three years later I was freelancing in San Francisco between jobs when I called a PR agency in Portland. She intercepted the call, ragging me unmercifully for standing her up. She was visiting San Francisco with a client the following week and we set up a meeting. I had no expectations, but decided to go in with an open mind. I had grown up a bit since standing her up for superficial reasons and decided that it didn't matter if she weighed a lot or if she had an abysmal fashion sense.

She had lied about her appearance, meeting her I saw a very attractive, dynamic, well spoken woman. We made plans to meet later for drinks but she cancelled, promising to get together in the future.

I flew up to Portland in December and we spent New Year's in San Jose. We commuted for a while until I moved to Portland in September. We got married the following month.

I had met a Beatle, no small feat, so I figured marriage would be a breeze after that.

Once in Portland, there were enough freelance assignments to keep me busy. Most were product oriented, where I'd review a computer or a software program or write about an ongoing trend. Throughout, I preferred the people oriented stories, where someone was using technology in a new way or was particularly interesting to begin with.

COMDEX was a twice yearly voyage, where I'd go to Las Vegas in the fall and Atlanta or Chicago in the spring to write product stories and seek out new assignments. The market changed after the fall 1992 event, which was pretty much where music, art and computers made their first intelligible connection. There followed a three-year period of chaos and confusion, ending with the conclusion that the Internet was the best option.

It took place in the Thomas and Mack Center, a basketball arena, and was dubbed "The Grand Scientific Musical Theater," attracting musicians and computer people to present a multimedia show meant to signal a new direction. Which boiled down to music and flashing lights, more or less.

It was a benefit for the National Center for Missing and Exploited Children, but it was never really clear where the money came from and how it was distributed since most people got in for free.

As a journalist I was allowed to walk up to anyone and ask any question. Being a member of the press set me aside from all the phonies and hanger-ons. That was the theory, since many of them treated me like one of those fans. Which I was.

Six weeks before the show I got a call from a publicist about the event, telling me "there will be lots of great musicians that I'm sure you'll like." Since I've always bucked the taste trend I was pretty sure she was wrong, especially considering the losers that usually played trade shows.

She swore me to secrecy but let on who was supposed to show up. Todd Rundgren and Graham Nash. Two for two already. Jon Anderson from Yes; and Flo and Eddie from the Turtles. Edgar Winter. And she was trying to get Peter Gabriel to commit.

A few days before leaving she called me in a panic. *Billboard* was looking for someone to cover the show. Could I possibly fit it into my schedule? Yes, please.

The last pre-show call had to do with the house band. Doobie Brother Skunk Baxter. Session musicians Mike Finnegan, Leland Sklar and Jim Keltner. John Entwistle from The Who. Now that was cool, but I wasn't sure what connection he had to multimedia and technology.

Not much, it turns out. At a pre-show reception I asked Entwistle why he was there; he said he didn't know, that someone asked him to come and he had nothing to do. He looked at me balefully and turned away, reminiscent of my little backstage Who adventure twenty-two years before.

The center of attention was a mullet-powered whirlwind named Scott Page, a saxophonist who was working as a multimedia developer. The idea was to put on a show that featured state-of-the-art light and sound, the most complicated technology up to that point.

"This is where Silicon Valley and Hollywood first came together," Page recalled recently. "The idea was to bring together the greatest technology at that time, and from that point on things started to take off. There were a lot of contacts and connections that came out of this."

Pink Floyd and Genesis lent their lighting gear. The lights were driven by Silicon Graphics machines, creating 3D animations throughout the theater. It would have been a lot for an attentive audience to digest, but the attendees were anything but. COMDEX parties were created for networking, and the cook-off was already the place to meet up with key people. This mission was not to be derailed by flashing lights and loud noises.

Music is only a small part of what makes a concert great or not. Sometimes a stellar performance falls flat, if you've taken the wrong drugs or your mind is on something else. Or it can be like this night, where only passable music shines because of the people who are there, or if some other factor makes the show a once-in-a-lifetime thing.

Here, this combination would never occur again. Peter Gabriel turned up as a spectator, and it was a fun game to watch people walk toward his table and then turn away in fear. Full of myself, I sat at the table where he was conversing with Rundgren. Gabriel spoke to someone, who looped around and asked who I was and why I was there. When I identified myself as press he said I could stay, as long as I didn't say a word or write anything down. I left. What was the point?

After the show all the cool people gathered in the basement. COMDEX parties are all alike, but this one stood out due to attendees who weren't selling modems. Nash, Rundgren, Entwistle, Jon Anderson, and Flo and Eddie. Peter Gabriel. All there and available for small talk.

I went up to the dessert tray, where two dress-for-success women were pointing at a guy in the corner. He was wearing a gray suit, a fedora and shades. There was music and he was moving rhythmically in between two platinum women.

"So is that Jack Nicholson or what?" Dress asked Success.

"We should go up and talk to him," Success said.

"You can, but he's probably a weirdo," Dress said. "Did you see him in *Batman*? I heard that it was pretty close to who he really is."

What could I lose? I'd already been dismissed by Entwistle and Gabriel, so I might as well aim higher. I walked up to him with my notebook and introduced myself as a journalist.

I asked a few questions but his answers were vague and noncommittal. No quotes here; he doesn't seem to know where he is or why he's here. Like Entwistle.

He stopped moving and became serious, looking me in the eye. Maybe I would get a decent quote after all.

"Let me tell you, Charlie, that things aren't always what they seem." His voice had changed and didn't sound like himself at all.

I pondered this quote for a minute and understood where I was and who I wasn't with. He wasn't Jack Nicholson, he told me, and the real Jack would let him alone as long as he doesn't give any interviews.

I said, "Nice meeting you," and walked away, embarrassed. I swore that people were looking at me, knowing that I'd been conned.

The concert itself was unremarkable and the attempts to blend it with technology were clumsy and misdirected. But the partnerships forged that night moved the process through the lean times until the Internet took over and changed all the combinations.

When I hit sent the finished review the sun was rising:

The repertoire included some hits ("Teach Your Children," "Happy Together"), some reinterpretations (Rundgren's medley of Marvin Gaye tunes), and some experiments (a new classical piece written by Anderson and performed with the Las Vegas Symphony).

The performances were accompanied by live graphics created on the spot on high-end work stations, often in close choreography to the music.

There were several large projection screens and many monitors through-out the hall. Often, the effects were too large for the eye to comprehend.

Representatives of the PC world and a number of noted musicians mixed well into the night, discussing the blend of their respective indus-tries and looking for ways to combine the right-brain linear creativity of the PC folks with the left-brained warmth of rock 'n' roll.

Micrografx president J. Paul Grayson said the event cost between $250,000 and $500,000, although a true estimate was impossible because of the volume of donated time and money.

Said Alan Parsons, who worked the soundboards, "If this wasn't a benefit, it would have been impossible to put on."

While the show allowed no more audience participation than a stan-dard concert, "interactivity" became the evening's backstage buzzword. The participants spoke of soon-to-be-available media products that would allow listeners to take a greater part in the process.

Rundgren, for instance, said his next album will allow the listener with CD-I hardware to alter tempo, length, and sequence of his material. The nearly complete album, called No World Order, *contains 355 pieces that are stitched together by the listener from an included "database" of 1,500 segments.*

Producer Bob Ezrin, who added advice and direction to the show, was excited about the possibilities of multimedia as a delivery medium. "The PC is focused on the marrying of information and entertainment," he said. "It's finally cost-effective to do this, and the change will be more dramatic than that brought about from either the CD or video."

Gabriel, who watched most of the show from a table along the periphery, was mum about the details of his own interactive title but said it would be available in 1993. Of interactivity, he said: "It carries the music to a new level and will allow the user to become part of the process beyond where they can just respond to it passively."

Nash said he planned to take a multimedia solo show on the road in 1993, which will use video, audio, and graphics to present a kinetic autobiography. "My previous complaint about computers was they were too glittery and sharp. We need to find a way to add content to the technology, but talk about the things that are more real. A song that matters comes from the heart."

Rundgren concurred, saying, "The rules haven't changed. You still have to make good music."

COMDEX always drew people out of context with technology but somehow persuaded to shill computer peripherals. *Gilligan Island*'s Bob Denver. Baseball phenom Reggie Jackson. Actors Robert Urich and Shelley Duvall, all pushing products they barely understood.

Once I was walking through a group of exhibits when Joan Rivers came up to me and asked "can we talk" about a network product. I believed her completely. Joan Rivers was not part of my world and I had no clear perception about her position in the celebrity pecking order. It was not beyond the realm of possibility that she was hanging around a trade show selling software. When I asked for an autograph she demurred, saying there were rules for celebrity impersonators.

Impersonators? Shit.

One year I went to a Toshiba event in the Hilton's Star Trek lounge, where Richie Havens appeared in the Star Trek Lounge at the Las Vegas Hilton and sang a few songs from the Woodstock Festival. I talked to him before the set. After every question his publicist broke in and said, "You can't ask him that."

"What's the difference between COMDEX and Woodstock?" I said.

"No bud at COMDEX, Richie said.

"You can't print that," the publicist said.

"Watch me," I replied.

Two years later there were products, but it seemed like every one had nothing to do with the other. I was in it for the music and the musicians, and was able to get past their structure. They were all patterned after computer games, where you trolled through secret chambers to find hidden treasures.

These products were flawed on a conceptual level. They were intended to continue the conversation between artists and listeners, but had more in common with a computer game than an LP jacket. It wasn't a favorable comparison. A CD ROM would make you dig down deep for exclusive information, while it was hidden in plain sight on an album cover.

And I hated games, in the same way I hated basketball in junior high.

The idea was embraced by the old guard, presumably looking to regain some of the contact lost with the LP's practical extinction. Bob Dylan took us to a Greenwich Village folk club where he had begun, along with a seat at a posh 1993 show. Prince allowed people into his purple lair. The Rolling Stones invited people into a "Voodoo Lounge," where one could click on a door and meet all the band's blues influences.

Peter Gabriel checked in with *Xplora 1*, an audio-video dissection of his then-new *Us* album, which allowed the listener to select various exotic instruments and hear them together. There was also the opportunity to riffle through a virtual suitcase, where you could examine various memorabilia. David Bowie's *Jump* employed his recent single, "Jump They Say," to create different versions of a rock video and save them to floppy disc. The product suffered from the fact that "Jump" was one of his least interesting songs, and that the price was $49.95.

Prince went all out with *Prince Interactive*. This was a fancy package that included two exclusive tracks and, as the press release stated, "a labyrinth of 11 different environments and unlimited passageways for the user to explore." This was during the artist's abandonment of his given name in favor of an unpronounceable symbol to protest alleged record-company malfeasance, so part of the trip was gathering eleven different parts of the symbol. Assembling the pieces yielded an exclusive video.

Todd Rundgren unleashed *No World Order*, with the music broken into 1,500 short segments that could be randomly rearranged or sequenced by the user. For the length of the disc you were Todd's producer. The end product was definitely Rundgren, reflecting his wacky instrumental side rather than his more commercial stuff. The music, though, wasn't his best.

It was all an experiment, we told ourselves, so it didn't matter if the content was hardly compelling. Aside from a searchable database of Dylan's lyrics, you wouldn't load these discs more than once. Dubious graphics was one drawback, along with the fact that one could listen to an entire LP side in the time that it took images to load.

As for people who actually liked games, the graphics weren't fancy enough and the pace was too slow.

The titles improved somewhat after the release of the more multimedia-inclined Windows 95, which also represented a bump for Internet use. Musicians were quick to establish their own web pages, which eventually allowed them to post pictures, video, audio, words and anything else needed to bring them closer to fans, or keep them at a distance.

Peter Noone, best known as the lead singer for Herman's Hermits, was an early adopter. Since there were no rules, he made up his own. His daily personal posts fell between autobiography and cockeyed revisionist history.

Noone, who was then in his early fifties, had been a pop star since age seventeen. Back then he was the object of fan clubs, which he said provided the web pages' ancestor.

"When I was touring back in the sixties, fans would send letters to my management or record company and it would take months to get to me, if I would read them at all," he said. "Today I get them right away, and if someone wants to hear a particular song at a particular concert I can fill their request."

He recalled ironic advice once offered to him by John Lennon: "Fans are great, if you don't let them breathe on you." This applied as a web page was the ultimate way to get close to people without actually meeting them.

The resulting web pages satisfied the need for providing interactivity to the listener. We could stop pining for the LP jacket, as the web provided all of its missing aspects.

"We're seeing the birth of the musician business, taking the place of the music business," occasional Grateful Dead lyricist John Perry Barlow told me in 2000. "Musicians are now in the position to interact with the audience without the intermediaries who have made money from music without contributing anything."

Like every other business that sought an online presence, musician web pages went through a difficult birth. Soon enough, these sites moved into adolescence and adulthood. Today every artist has a slick web page, which along with other online sources provides everything you ever wanted to know, and more.

This is probably a good thing. If we want to know about a musician, we know where to look. Fans now have the illusion of closeness, as every page has a contact" screen. The quality of this interaction depends on the artist's responsiveness and the fan's questions, but it is theoretically possible.

Artist web pages have come a long way, with the Internet evolving into an album's liner notes with the steps worth noting. Even as vinyl has returned, web pages have evolved into a place where people can go, if enjoyment of the music is not quite enough.

Telethony

——

April 2003, Bainbridge Island, Washington

YOU ARE JUST SHY OF turning fifty, and nothing is as you had imagined. You live in a posh suburb across the water from Seattle, watching a once-lucrative freelance writing career collapse. You are lucky to be married to a woman who owns her own business and can occasionally throw you a writing assignment, which you complete and see it translate into an exchange for room and board, so you feel like you are adding something. Not so lucky is that she is in the third year of Stage IV breast cancer.

You two didn't like the same music and it is possible she never took the whole rock experience as seriously. When someone has cancer, you don't force them to accompany you to Todd Rundgren and you search out opportunities that will help her to forget the disease for a little while. So you don't complain when you land tickets for a Tina Turner/Joe Cocker show and she decides at the last minute to stay home.

Jerry Lewis, Seattle 2003

There is never a guarantee in this life, but when she says she wants to attend a celebrity event you set out to make it happen, even if your affection for that particular celebrity, Jerry Lewis, is roughly equivalent to hers for Neil Young.

Your parents didn't much like Jerry Lewis. They never took you to his movies or watched him on TV. Instead you got a steady dose of *West Side Story* and Peter, Paul and Mary, along with classical stuff that didn't hold your attention. During trips to New York City your grandmother would take you to see anything you wanted, and you always chose James Bond or a gladiator movie over any comedy playing at the time.

Your wife grew up in a different house, somewhere in the Midwest. Jerry Lewis was one of the greats, she said, and not only in France or Libertyville. You then try to become closer by familiarizing yourself with the nuances of your new wife's taste, which involves watching several of his movies together. There are some hilarious moments but the movies remind you of Woody Allen films that start out strong but lose their way about forty-five minutes in. Your wife laughs right before the funny parts, which causes you to miss them entirely.

During the cancer treatment, you haven't given Lewis a passing thought. Your time is mostly spent looking for work, maintaining the house, and driving to chemo every Tuesday. Each time you escort her to the ward and then walk to the newsstand for a stack of gossip magazines that you read together until it's time to remove the tubes.

On this particular day, something catches your eye on the bulletin board. A notice advertising a session on pain management, taking place in the hospital auditorium and featuring Lewis. In person. You hurry back to the chemo station, running up the stairs to deliver the news. Your wife doesn't quite believe you, which is fair enough because we've spent half our marriage faking each other out. Anticipating this, you had brought a copy of the flier, which you now must tack back up before anybody notices.

There is a health-related website that has expressed interest in your writing but no assignments have materialized. They like the idea so you call the public-relations department of the event's sponsoring company and learn that Mr. Lewis may be available for a chat after the next day's event.

You have been to enough of these things to know there are certain rules. One is to arrive early to get a good seat. Another is that your past heroes look and act differently than at their prime. You arrive an hour early to the small auditorium expecting a line, but you are the only person there. You stake out three seats in the third row and await your wife's arrival, along with her friend.

But there is no one in the auditorium aside from the setup crew and a woman on a cell phone who is saying, "He is a lot like Jim Carrey, only older." When Lewis arrives, "older" doesn't begin to cover it. You are waiting in the hall when they wheel him into an adjacent waiting room, tethered to an oxygen tank. He is easily twice the size as in "The Nutty Professor," which you had watched the night before. You find the PR woman to ask about the interview but she is noncommittal. It seems impolite to push.

It begins with a brief series of old film clips and then Jerry arrives. He walks up to the stage and sits down to applause, a bit more restrained than what you expect but this is a hospital. Your wife pays no mind to this; she is clapping eagerly and whistling loudly. She is wearing a straight-red-hair wig from the Raquel Welch collection.

You recall later that Jerry worked with Raquel Welch on *Hollywood Palace*. Jerry stops for a second and looks straight at your wife.

"Is your name Valerie?" he asks.

She shoots back, "It could be."

You are aware that in this wig she bears a slight resemblance to Valerie Perrine. You're not sure if Jerry and Valerie ever worked together, but Madeline Kahn, who has the same vibe, starred with him in *Slapstick*.

He soon gets to the point, that people don't need to live with chronic pain. He ties in his own story, how his performing his own stunts on a 1965 movie led to a permanent injury and an addiction to painkillers. It got so bad that he came near to committing suicide but was saved by a fortuitous meeting with a pain management specialist. He ended up with an electronic implant that short-circuits pain impulses and allows him a normal life.

Although what is "normal" for Lewis is never made clear. His pulmonary fibrosis required prednisone, which caused the dramatic weight gain. So if it isn't one thing it's another.

"They make pain management second-class," Jerry says at the end. "Right now, a lot of the doctors don't know any more about managing pain than they guy who's parking your car." He calls for oxygen and takes a long draw, then admits that "sometimes I do this for dramatic effect."

Once he leaves the stage his face and posture changes, as if the power was shut down. He is wheeled into the small room and you realize the there will be no interview. The PR lady comes out to explain but you stop her with a wave of your hand. "I know he can't talk now, but do you think I can get an autograph?"

The paper in hand, you return home. Your wife is so happy she allows you to drive and is not miffed that you did not get to ask the questions she suggested. You frame the autograph, along with a picture taken at the event. It is crisp and clear, and you marvel about what you can do with home-based photo printers.

You print out a few of the shots taken of Jerry. While they are clear around the edges they seem out of proportion because his head is so large. You play around with Photoshop and superimpose his face on a picture of the moon, at which point it takes on its proper dimension.

Weeks pass. She is in a better mood than usual mostly because you are planning a trip to Ireland, to rent a house for a week and soak in the countryside. You are relieved that it will not be one of those vacations in which you see five cities in seven days. She talks of Jerry often and talked about sending him a fan letter, saying how much he was inspired by him and how his in-the-face-of-adversity demeanor had elevated her mood.

You write a story about the event, but since it lacked the promised interview the website felt it wasn't worth publishing. Jerry's press tour gets a lot of attention and one night he appears on *Conan O'Brien* and you set the timer on the VCR. Watching it the next day your wife is again inspired and writes him a letter, including how after the presentation she was motivated to explore pain-management options at the hospital and found there was a department devoted to that function. Which no one had told her about.

I'm sure glad that Jerry Lewis had the strength to get out of his wheelchair and fly up to Seattle to help us patients know how to get help from their own hospital, she wrote.

You paste the finished letter into an email and send it to the PR lady who acknowledges its receipt, agrees to pass it on, "but won't make any promises" about a response.

Two days later there is a brusque message on the answering machine: "Please call Jerry Lewis," with a 619 area code. Your wife doesn't call right away and then Jerry calls again, calling her a "little creep" for not responding. Over the next few weeks they talk quite a bit and you even chat a time or two, but you are reserved and detached. This particular celebrity connection does not belong to you, even if it is clear that the story could be told and sold. You are not willing to attempt this, since it would mean writing down the truth about your home life and admitting feelings in public that you are not willing to disclose.

During the time before the Ireland trip, Jerry talks to your wife a few times a week. Her mood improves after each call, and beyond that her doctors notice an improvement in her attitude. It doesn't quite translate into test results, but at least the numbers aren't getting any worse.

You walk into a room and she hangs up the phone. You aren't threatened by the relationship because you know he's married. They talk a lot, and pretty soon you get the feeling that she's cheering him up as much as he is cheering her up. One night she tells him a joke. "This guy goes to the doctor and the doctor said 'I have bad news and worse news. You have cancer. And you have Alzheimer's.' So the guy thinks for minute and says 'At least I don't have cancer.' " There was a silence and she hangs up the phone.

"He didn't really think it was all that funny," she said.

You think that the joke is pretty good, and have been telling it for weeks. But you wouldn't have told it to Jerry any more than you would have played Paul McCartney one of your own songs if he came to visit.

You read about Jerry, watch several of his movies, and acknowledge his importance. You blame your parents because they didn't take you to these movies. You remember why you got into journalism as a teenager: to have the license to meet celebrities and ask them questions. To impress them, so they would like you. You realize that your wife, who doesn't believe in celebrities on pedestals and minimizes your choices, has accomplished your goals without trying.

The day before you leave for Ireland, your wife gets a call. This time it's not from Jerry but one of his people, with an invitation to fly down to LA on Labor Day for the MDA telethon. The flight and the hotel is paid for; there will be a car at the airport. Jerry would be honored if you would accept the invitation.

The hotel was really posh. The weather was clear and warm. You stayed in on Friday night and watched TV, lucking into a broadcast of *Mr. Saturday Night* that made you believe in coincidences. It is a fake biography of a fictional comedian, Buddy Young Jr., portrayed by Billy Crystal and with a short appearance by Jerry Lewis as himself.

On Saturday you sit by the pool and order omelets. There are people all around and you catch showbiz chatter from the next table, where the guy obviously knows Jerry well. He speaks with loud exaggeration. The emotion is clear but you make an effort to tune him out. He is some kind of star and he needs his privacy. He's bald and his head has the tanned texture of a walnut.

He cracks another joke and someone calls him "Norm," but you still don't know who he is. Until later at the telethon he is introduced as Norm Crosby, whom you saw several times on the *Ed Sullivan Show* while waiting for the Beatles or the Rolling Stones. You remember his act, how he would mix up words that sounded alike but had different meanings.

He does that a few times here, but you don't really pay attention because you are transfixed by his hair. You know it's a wig and you wonder why it was crafted to include a receding headline. You wonder why he picked that particular spot on his head as the point where hair ends and baldness begins.

After breakfast you hail a cab to the studio. You tell the cabbie where you are going and how you got there, and he tells you that Jerry Lewis is a wonderful, generous person. He didn't know what to expect when Lewis got into his cab the previous year, so he became tongue-tied. But that didn't last long because Lewis started talking, the cabbie started talking back, and the notion of celebrity disappeared. The story ended the only way possible, with Lewis leaving a huge tip.

The cabbie asks what you've done so far and you tell him, mentioning the posh breakfast and the previous night's movie. Which the cabbie had seen several times and loved. "That Buddy Young Jr.," the cabbie said. "Such a comedian. Such a mensch. And Billy Crystal did a great portrayal." As you open your mouth your wife squeezes your thigh. Hard. You realize that it might be time to stop correcting people.

You get to the studio about an hour before the show, channeled into a small room that was set up as a commissary with long tables and a buffet. The furnishings were almost identical to the setup you visited at the hospital the week before but the food was extraordinary. Beef Stroganoff. Huge salads. Sushi rolls with white or brown rice. You fill a plate and head to a table and sit down next to a group of telethon staffers. Who turned out to be teachers, railing against the California school system.

They are seated on either side of your wife, talking simultaneously, which gave her a weird stereo effect. One of them mentioned the criminal justice system, at which time she began reciting, "In the criminal justice system the people are protected by two separate but equally important groups…."

The teacher people listened until they realize your wife was parroting the *Law & Order* intro, and they cracked up.

It turns out you are on the A list, so the ushers respectfully walk you down a driveway into the studio and seat you about ten rows back from the main stage. This consists of a large wooden desk on the left and an open performance space at the right. For most of the evening Jerry is sitting at the desk while Ed McMahon is on a microphone at the far right.

You aren't kept waiting long. Since this is live TV it needs to start at the top of the hour so you are prepared. There is a ruckus on the ramp, caused by a motorcycle gang led by a huge guy in leathers and a helmet. Jerry making his entrance, you think, but it evolves into a perfect misdirection. Jerry emerges, in a tuxedo, from somewhere else.

He settles at the desk and brings out a few people. You've heard of all of them, but not for a very long time. Don Rickles. Jack Jones. Patti Page. And Norm Crosby, of course. There is chatter that Nancy Sinatra is on the schedule. But you have no idea whether that will occur in ten minutes or ten hours.

For a while you marvel at the opportunity to see celebrities in repose, but even this loses its luster considering the celebrities in question.

By this time you have been hammered by the message, to contribute money to the cause, and you make a note to do so today, tomorrow and every year from now on. You wonder why more people aren't involved, more people you've heard of or care about. You think of a line from a recent movie: "If you build it, they will come." No one is going to go anywhere for some of these people. You wonder about the big names, what better things they have to do than come down here and wave the muscular-dystrophy flag.

As everyone's energy, including your own, operates in waves, the only person in the room with unflagging energy was Jerry himself. Your wife gets tired all the time, so you are surprised that it took her three hours before leaning over and grimacing, telling you it was time to leave.

At the next commercial break you get up to go and flag down Jerry's manager, Claudia, to tell her you are on your way out. She goes all business and says, "You have to meet Jerry," so you move reluctantly toward the large desk.

As a gift you have prepared a Rubik's Cube of six edited images, including Jerry as Napoleon and on the face of Mount Rushmore in place of Lincoln. Jerry beams when he received the gift, and meets your wife for the first time, and reminds you of the picture that you didn't include. The one where his face covered the expanse of a full moon.

You struggle to get a picture of your wife and Jerry in the same frame, using a digital camera that you have never figured out. You can't get everyone looking in the same direction but there is a professional photographer snapping away. Considering your treatment so far, you expect a signed eight-by-ten print will end up in your mailbox soon enough.

The lights started flashing and we were ushered out. Jerry gave your wife a hug and a kiss on the cheek. You go back to the room and turn on the TV to see an amorphous Nancy Sinatra singing with a picture of her father in the background. The sound is muted, the way you left it before, and you aren't motivated to turn it back on. You had heard that she was going to sing a song written by the guys in U2, and expected something a bit more energetic and kinetic, maybe even "These Boots Are Made for Walkin'" redux. Nothing that exciting is going on here, so you flip the channel. Which ends up as an encore presentation of "Mr. Saturday Night."

You go home to return to normal life, which becomes less so. There is no picture of the moment but it hardly matters. You don't need a picture to prove that the moment really existed. In November you begin a new job, working on a small weekly, where you get to cover land use and local government.

After a few weeks you play around with some desktop-publishing software and develop a twenty-page booklet to commemorate the occasion. You include your wife's letter to Jerry, pictures, narratives and quotes from friends and doctors detailing how Jerry had lit up your wife's life. You print up six copies. All of them have a color cover of which you are proud, but one copy has color pictures on the inside as well.

One night your wife gets irritated and tears the color book in half. You're a bit hurt, but she apologizes and you decide to give her a break. What would be the point of doing otherwise?

Your wife talks to Jerry a few times after the telethon but the calls taper off. You don't get a Christmas card, or something for her birthday, for which Jerry knows the date. Like the absent picture this matters little. He had come into your lives and lit everything up, bringing a laughter and optimism that was too long absent in your marriage.

And he had moved on. Jerry was known for absurd comedies but this felt more like a cowboy movie, the one about the gunfighter who passes through town and sets all the wrong things right: "Who was that funny man? I meant to thank him."

Your wife's doctors abandon hope and she enters home hospice. A few weeks later you realize her days are few so you give Jerry a call using the number left on the answering machine the previous year, which you have never erased. "It looks like she doesn't have much longer," you say into the machine. "If you have the time to call that would be great. If not I thank you for coming into her life because your presence took away some of the pain of the last year."

You listen for the phone, hoping to intercept the call. You were never comfortable talking to Jerry because you are a part-time celebrity journalist and using access to this celebrity seems like cheating. This time it would be nice to be able to tell Jerry that your wife has lost her center and is subject to mood swings.

Several hours later you take a nap and a shower, only to learn that Jerry had called and that it did not go well. She had told Jerry that she was being held captive, that everyone in the house was out to drive her crazy, hasten her death and steal her money. She calmed down and handed the phone to one of the nurses, who thought she'd have the opportunity to explain your wife was safe and that such disassociation was common. But Jerry was no longer on the line.

When she dies about a week later, you don't think to let Jerry know, since he's already moved on. It might have been different if he used email, which you were using quite a lot to keep people posted since you don't have to hear people's shock at the news or their sympathetic responses. You know they mean well, but if you hear the words "thoughts and prayers" one more time you will probably attack somebody.

As Jerry moves on, you do as well. A year later you've had no urge to watch his old movies, or even make a special effort to see his talk-show appearances. Eight years later he appears in a monologue show at a local casino and you make some halfhearted efforts to sell the piece to a few local papers. You are sure that if there was an assignment you could land an interview because you still have the phone number that Jerry left on your machine years before. But you don't care enough to develop a convincing sales pitch. The editors you contact sense this and send you rejection notices, or don't respond at all.

The lack of effort has to do with an inability to write honestly. You cannot approach this as just another celebrity interview because of the personal trauma tied into your interaction with Jerry. If you were to interview him, you would certainly share this past and that would require more openness than you are prepared to share at that point. Someday when you are ready to open up you will write all of it down in an honest way.

Time Travel

———

September 2006: Wheelchair Legends: How Some Rockers Grow Old Gracefully and Others Do Not

PUYALLUP, WASHINGTON—ARE THERE GATHERINGS like this anywhere outside of the modern American West? A million people come to a converted dusty field over a period of two weeks, to jump on wild rides, stuff themselves with trans-fats and get up close and personal with various combinations of livestock. They walk away with cheap souvenirs, from promotional backpacks that smell like diesel to magnets that look like metal testicles and whirr like crickets as you throw them in the air.

Additionally, audiences can get up close to the formerly famous, those who once required a long wait and big bucks in order to be part of their scene. Every evening there is a fairground musical attraction, someone either on their way up or down. Carrie Underwood, the current American Idol, is the biggest name, while the Beach Boys (or more precisely, the Beach Boy) will play here next week. Tonight we have come to see the Rock N' Roll Legends, remnants of four 1960s bands (Herman's Hermits, the Monkees, the Turtles and the Grass Roots).

We get the real Peter Noone, not the embarrassing mess of a revival band that features the original drummer and three substitutes. And you can't beat the price or the wait. Anyone who pays regular fair admission can witness competent versions of songs they once loved, sung with a moderate amount of authenticity by the original voices. For fifteen dollars more they can get a seat up close.

"It's great to be out here in the open air," said Turtles lead singer Howard Kaylan, with a dig at the alternate venue for this type of show. "It sure beats singing at one of those Indian casinos."

I Was So Much Older Then

"Authenticity" is the most important word tonight, along with "ambivalence." In their heyday, these bands lived or died by the authenticity sword. They all strived to be different and original. Derivativeness was the kiss of death. Remember the outcry when we heard that the Monkees didn't play their own instruments. At the time, the Turtles, Beach Boys and even the Beatles didn't exactly raise their hands and admit they were guilty of the same crime.

Today, absolute authenticity is not an option. Almost every 1960s band has at least one dead member. You then eliminate those who hate each other's guts, or those who once played their own instruments but can't anymore.

On this tour we have the original voices, with pretty much the same guitar-bass-keyboard-drums accompaniment. Since there are no absolute rules—or they change with each listener—these performers can get away with anything that sounds good. Some audience members won't even require that much.

Ambivalence comes from the fact that we don't really care if these guys are the originals or not. These songs evoked a feeling; a place and time. And those in the audience who weren't there the first time aren't likely to complain—or even notice—how it doesn't match the originals.

The best example of this authenticity slide is, again, the Beach Boys. Mike Love is the only original member, and still sings lead on many recognizable hits. But ringers perform the Wilson brothers' parts well enough. Noone, who is himself in constant argument with a former band member who co-opts the Hermits' name, says the Beach Boys have never sounded better live.

So what happens when Love, at sixty-five, no longer wants to tour? Four original members are already missing, with no apparent protest aside from critics and snobs. Soon enough, Love will be replaced by someone who sings in his general register and the band will continue. This is not without precedent; jazz bands often tour for decades under the names of their dead founders.

Grass Rudeness

I spent much of the mid-1960s listening to the Monkees and Herman's Hermits. I bought their albums, bestowing them with the same intensity and dedication as my just-olders were devoting to The Who and the Kinks. I thought the Monkees' *Headquarters* was actually superior to its two predecessors. And while I still have never had any opportunity to view a movie called *Hold On*, I can attest that the Hermits' soundtrack was definitely keen.

But I would feel a lot better today had I followed the trajectory of the Grass Roots. At the time I thought they were pretty lame, compared to what else was going on. Their singles were good enough, but not so much that I would ever buy one. I was, after all, twelve. There was a lot of really great music coming out every week, and it was another two years before I could afford *Buffalo Springfield Again*.

Upon hearing of this traveling show with Noone, Micky Dolenz, Turtle principals Mark Volman and Kaylan, and Grass Root Rob Grill, I set out to tell the story to those who might still care. But my interview request was a bit too honest, asking to talk to all but adding, "I can do without Grill, given a choice." Tactless and rude perhaps, but I felt talking with him would waste everyone's time. After all, both Rob and I are over fifty, where the time supply isn't infinite.

The note is distributed to all the artists. Noone and Dolenz respond immediately, with the Turtles' Mark Volman coming in a few hours later. Then a phone message:

"Hello, I represent Rob Grill and we got a letter here, and it says 'I can do without talking to Rob Grill, given the choice.' So we'll just take that choice out of your hands. I want to thank you for your interest, or lack thereof. You can call this number if you want to talk to me, or if you want to talk to Mr. Grill. Who is me."

He is still pissed when I return the call. I apologize, but he is unmoved. I had no class, he said. He hangs up. I dial again. He will not relent. He says no one will let me into the show. No one will talk to me. And I shouldn't bother him again.

Noone and Volman stay true to their word, each chatting on the phone for more than an hour. But Dolenz backs out. His representative writes, saying, "His schedule does not allow." When I push, he admits "that whole mess with Rob Grill kind of screwed it up."

When *Sgt. Pepper* emerged in June 1967 I tucked away the newly released *Headquarters* pretty much forever. These past few weeks would have been a lot more stress-free if I had then sacrificed the Grass Roots' *Let's Live for Today*.

You Really Like Me

The musicians' view of themselves is alternately profound and humorous.

"These four acts are some of the strongest visual acts you will see," Volman said. "They are survivors. They have been able to, year after year, make a good living. They have put their children through college. They have owned homes. They are strong businessmen. They are real professionals."

"You can always tell the guys who weren't in the original band," Noone said. "Because they can't read the set list."

Noone's set list has some heft. He had a long string of hits with the Hermits, some of which stand the test of time and some don't. Somewhere along the line he fell out of the spotlight, losing the focus of the general public while hanging on to a core of fans that insist he far surpasses any of his contemporaries. This, like his continuous performance of old hits is not unique—although his enthusiasm is.

While we may not think of Noone in the same breath as John, Paul, Mick or Pete, he once breathed the same air. And they all keep in touch.

"It's a survival thing," he said. "Like an old regiment, or a platoon. But we aren't all like Fabian, where we look at each other and say 'You look marvelous.' You can't look at Keith Richards and say that he looks great. But it's great that we are still here."

Most Hermits-era bands borrowed blues idioms and fed it back to the Americans whose countrymen invented it in the first place. But there was nothing bluesy about the Hermits. Their music was evenly divided between

American "oldies," English music-hall tunes (or imitations thereof), and new songs by composers like Graham Gouldman and Gerry Goffin-Carole King.

"We wanted to do songs that were different," Noone said. "We couldn't do 'Roll Over Beethoven' because the Beatles did it, and they did it better than us. We couldn't do 'Love Potion #9' because the Searchers did it. So we took some English music-hall songs, and some that sounded like English music-hall, like 'Mrs. Brown'."

Like the folk era that immediately preceded, bands often did the same songs. Both the Hermits and Freddie and the Dreamers did "I Understand." The Hermits shared "Where Were You When I Needed You" with the Grass Roots. Hit singles were a crapshoot. Gouldman's "Bus Stop" was a hit for the Hollies instead of the Hermits, even as their versions sounded about the same through a transistor radio. And the Hermits sweetened up the Kinks' "Dandy" and Donovan's "Museum," which were basically rescued album tracks.

Noone's real cultural contribution didn't occur until the late 1990s, when he invented blogging. While all the former rock stars were fiddle-farting with the Internet and punching out identical promotional web pages, Noone was writing down his every thought for public consumption. He peppered the site with reminisces, which in every other decade would have turned into a forgettable book. He added a healthy dose of fantasy: his "Club Me" shows him taking on personas like "Peteloaf" and "The Very Reverend Sun Lung Noone."

When I first visited www.peternoone.com in 1999 I was struck by the whimsical detail. A lot of these remembrances wouldn't work in a book, as they were mostly charming lies. We got a trip into Noone's imagination, which may be a little more fertile than your own. Besides, he met John Lennon. And Stevie Wonder, when he was Little.

Consider this entry, about his visit to Detroit's Motown studio in 1965:

I was sort of nonplussed that (Wonder) actually 'knew' my songs, and was so comfortable with himself, but off he went singing 'Mrs. Brown You've Got a Lovely Daughter' with the most perfect impersonation of me I have ever heard. Being a quick-witted sort of chap, I told him that I was a huge fan of his work, but hadn't got my harmonica with me but, that by an incredible quirk of circumstance I had just purchased his latest album and that I had it with me right there under my arm.

He was duly impressed and signed it and it is in my personal hall of shame and funny things I have done. I would have told him the truth eventually but my Mum told me it was all right to be funny if it didn't hurt anyone's feelings and I never got another opportunity to tell Marvin Gaye that Little Stevie Wonder had signed all over his face.

True? Maybe. Worth reading? Absolutely. We don't need another rock-star bio that provides a different viewpoint of something we already know. Noone's writing is much like he talks, eyes wide and free of guile. He isn't really name-dropping, because he's still jazzed about these stories.

How John Lennon once told him that fans are great, if they don't breathe on you. How Jimmy Page asked to play on the Hermits' records and can be heard on "Silhouettes" and "Wonderful World." How David Bowie played what was to become "Hunky Dory," and Noone thought he "had discovered the new Paul McCartney, by accident." Of these, "Oh, You Pretty Things," was one of the last Hermits singles. Bowie was on the session, Noone recalls that "he was a fantastic pianist, but could only play on the black keys." And every time Noone sees Bowie, he again offers his keyboard services.

I tell Noone that I've never heard his version of "Pretty Things" and he erupts. "It's a great record!" he says as he asks for my email address. A moment later an MP3 arrives in my inbox. It's a worthy curiosity, but also quite clear why this wasn't a hit. It lacks both the reedy appeal of Hermits' records and the plaintive menace of Bowie's own version.

Hot for Teacher

Aware of the available options, Mark Volman earned a master's degree in his forties and is now a college professor, teaching history and music-business theory at Belmont University in Nashville. Classes are Tuesday and Thursday; he takes the Turtles out on the weekends.

"When we were seventeen years old we weren't really thinking about the business," Volman said. "We were doing this to make records, tour and meet girls. We wanted to do something that our parents didn't think we could do.

"There is not a big future for someone with a music degree. If you play the French horn, there aren't a lot of symphonies where you can work. In my class I teach kids about surviving in the business, in case their own music doesn't pan out."

Volman must be a blast in the classroom, but few of us will have the privilege firsthand. There is, of course, a website (www.askprofessorflo.com) that contains a portion of the syllabus and where you can (presumably) get your music business questions answered.

The Turtles' perfect single, "Happy Together," hasn't lost its luster. The band knew the song was great, but had no idea it would be so huge. While they would never complain, it's clear that it messed them up. The record company pushed for another song just like it, and withheld funds when it didn't come. They gave in once or twice ("Elenore," "You Showed Me") but their singles-band status eclipsed two wonderful albums, *The Turtles Present the Battle of the Bands* and the Ray Davies-produced *Turtle Soup*. At the time, the Kinks' latest was *Village Green Preservation Society*.

"I always thought we were pretty close to the Kinks," Volman said. "We didn't have the same edge, but we had the same songwriting philosophy." Davies didn't leave too obvious a mark on the album, although parts of 'How You Loved Me' tells us what Dave Davies would have sounded like back then if he sang on pitch.

They still perform "Happy Together" enthusiastically, but its transformation into a sing-along takes away its menacing overtones. Listen to the words; it seems to be less of a love song than a stalker's hymn.

"The words conjured up a lot of emotion for people who could not be where they wanted to be or with who they wanted to be with," Volman said. "People who were in Vietnam told me how that song brought them so close to feeling like they were home."

When I ask whether he would like to correct any mistakes he laughs and says, "That is the first good question you've asked me." But he goes on to say he wouldn't change a thing, aside from the producer's credit.

Today's Turtles are as much about comedy as music. Volman—rotund, with a wave of curls and a beatific, confused expression—always made us laugh. Kaylan, who has looked like an old guy for some time, spends his onstage time looking befuddled, especially during a routine where he proclaims "all of those bands in the sixties and seventies who had a few hits and you never knew who they were and then went away were us."

He rattles off several names, up to and including Nirvana and Britney Spears, until Volman stages an intervention and a more subdued Kaylan announced "apparently there has been some confusion. We were not the O'Jays."

From the opening "You Baby" to "Happy Together," they roll good-naturedly through their best-known hits. The renditions are faithful and competent, and they enjoy themselves immensely. There are a few odd spots, such as a version of "Gimme Some Lovin'" sung by the bass player. This is confusing, as the song had nothing to do with the Turtles. And a long buildup to what they call "our new record" ("This is an experiment. It could really suck. But we feel really at home here and hope you will enjoy this") turns out to be a version of Neil Young's "Cinnamon Girl."

"Really suck" becomes the evening's grand understatement. Saying this is a new song is a classic case of bait-and-switch. The audience applauds, but we already know it is peppered with a bunch of unparticular yahoos.

After "Happy Together," Volman and Kaylan walk through the crowd toward the merchandising station (everyone signs autographs after the show, another reason it is not like the old days). The first synthesized bits of *Who's Next* filters through the PA as the crowd offers roaming standing ovation. It's a poetic moment, right out of a hero movie. It's a bit hokey but only a real mope wouldn't cheer along.

Dolenz arrives to an instrumental version of the Monkees' theme song, then bounces straight into "Last Train to Clarksville." The sound is clear and his voice sounds great. He's covering the entire Monkees catalogue and not just what he sang. We get "A Little Bit Me, A Little Bit You," and an embarrassing version of Mike Nesmith's "Different Drum" sung by Micky's sister, Coco. She redeems herself with some deft vocal counterpoints on "Daydream Believer."

Dolenz is also the only one on the bill who looks appreciably different than the old days. With a beard, suit and hat, all black, he could be a rabbi or a salesman. While his vocal clarity is the best part of his set, he sings as well at sixty-one as twenty-one. He still isn't much of a drummer, but his 4/4 pounding is just right for "Mary Mary." The set list, however, disappoints. A lot of their songs—those performed by Dolenz—hold up well. But tonight, we don't get to hear "Saturday's Child," "For Pete's Sake" or "Porpoise Song"— the one Monkees track that qualifies as brilliant.

There are always unplayed songs that someone in the audience wants to hear, and package shows necessarily aim for the lowest common denominator. Still, they are onstage for thirty-five minutes or so, and it would be nice if they could play their best songs instead of falling back on perceived crowd-pleasers. Every piece of shtick squanders their time onstage. Dolenz gives his sister the chance to sing a song Mike Nesmith wrote for Linda Ronstadt, and even those who don't hate the performance will wonder how it fits in. And the Turtles' version of a Spencer Davis song sacrifices second-string hits or outstanding album tracks.

Enjoyment here requires abandoning certain of your standards. This ranges from the willingness to accept ingratiating need of some of the acts to read off their resumé, or the general tackiness that goes beyond finding gobs of ketchup on your chair. I may be a snob, but I dropped Dolenz's live CD like a hot coal when I noticed it misspelled one of the songs as "Plesant Valley Sunday." And even as these guys brag about their own history, they still get it wrong. After "It Ain't Me, Babe," Volman announces "that is a song that Bob Dylan wrote for us." Perhaps he was being facetious, but the audience didn't know the difference. This is how myths get started.

The rock-star manual says nothing about competing with carnival lights for the audiences' attention and submitting to hours of signing autographs on vinyl records that are older than many people there—although Noone makes the best of it. One t-shirt is an old-style shot of the Hermits, but with his face superimposed on all five players. As he signs a pile of shirts backstage he refers to the image as "five ten-inch Peters."

Noone also does the onstage shtick, tossing off irreverent imitations of Johnny Cash and Tom Jones. Still, he is the only one tonight who seems genuine, who really connects with and actually enjoys the music. Volman and

Kaylan make it clear they are goofing around, and Dolenz, while he sounds great, is a little aloof.

Perhaps this is a mathematical drawback. You would be hard-pressed to name Hermits other than Noone or those who backed Volman and Kaylan in the Turtles (OK, I can, but I'm not like everybody else). Dolenz, as one-fourth of a well-known group, inevitably calls attention to those who aren't there.

Noone is always laughing and running around, and at one point he grabs a stack of CDs and gives them to several kids (that is to say, those under fifteen) who are sitting near the front. This is a generous act, and some audience members think that the lady who is walking through the crowd selling the discs is giving them away.

Monkee Si, Monkee Deux

Volman attributes the failure to produce new music to closed-minded radio programmers. All the available outlets—pop radio, classic rock, satellite—would all show a lack of interest in a new Turtles or Hermits album. So many of them don't even try. If people want to hear the old stuff, that's what they'll get. Every ten years or so they may do a new live album of the old songs, just to be producing something.

Some have produced new music and placed clips on cookie-cutter web pages. Here, you learn that Peter Tork has chosen a form of acoustic blues that is almost immediately annoying. But there are few exceptions. Eric Burdon has released an album a year for three years, a live one with just two crowd-pleasers and two new blues rock masterpieces. *Soul of A Man* is especially pure; he seems to work the same mine as always. Except today he is a lot more consistent and in control. This album strikes the balance between who he is and who we want him to be. So Burdon actually recreates that part of the 1960s, when you would go to a concert to hear the new songs and they are as compelling as the old ones.

Noone, it turns out, often scolds Burdon for his onstage indulgences; saying that audiences want to hear the old songs as they remember them. Noone follows his own advice, mostly, until he stretches "I'm Henry the Eighth, I Am" into a punky ten-minute sing-along jam.

Dolenz's former bandmate, the perpetually cantankerous Mike Nesmith, isn't stuck in the past. The first thing you notice about his new album, *Rays*, is that it has nothing to do with that guy in the Monkees who played country for a while and had something to do with the beginnings of MTV. The vocals, when he decides to sing, sound a little like the Wool Hat guy but the rest of it is just too wild. It's cinematic, but too irritating to be ambient. It's a good choice for your iTunes, though; when it pops up there is an immediate, gleeful "What the hell is that?"

Right after Volman says how no one is interested in new Turtles music, he lets slip that his partner has released a new album earlier this year. Kaylan's *Dust Bunnies* is an odd affair; he's half screaming the words against an abrasive background, although it's not quite metal. Three quarters in I recognize one song, a slowed-down version of the Honeycombs' "Have I The Right." Further research (this is the disadvantage of downloading) finds that only one is an original, and the rest are covers of the most obscure songs from people like Tim Buckley, John Miles and Charles Aznavour. Some of it works, while other songs are so annoying that you can't get to the skip button fast enough.

Five days later I stumble into a club date featuring P.F. Sloan, who wrote at least five of the songs played at the fair. It is quite a different scene; instead of a suntanned, middle-aged mob we get a handful of graying hippies entertained in a small dark room by a sixty-year-old greaser. He opens with "Secret Agent Man" and plays it as if Dylan was having a go—in this case, dragging it out into several verses and blowing the harmonica between each one. He follows the opener with a few alternately boring and irritating new songs.

It gets better when he unleashes a quiet version of "You Baby," the buoyant opener to the Turtles' set days before. Even as the unplugged trend has lost its luster, this is a perfect balance: A familiar song stripped down to its essence; familiar yet new. He follows this with a subtle version of "Where Were You When I Needed You," far superior to the overwrought original Grass Roots version (on which, it is said, he sang lead).

If some old guy in dark glasses were to show up at any club and play "Eve of Destruction" and "Let's Live for Today," you would think it was a joke. Sloan gets away with this because he wrote the songs, and (on paper, at least) gets to take any liberties he wants. If you like these new versions you can take them home, on a cheaply produced CD for sale in the back. In this respect, the Sloan event is identical to the fair.

It is a continuous privilege how we can see the past greats in a small club, an open amphitheater or a casino playing songs from the old days. But it's also a mixed blessing, as sooner or later we dovetail back to the ideas of authenticity and quality—remembering when they were the same.

August 2007: Things aren't what they used to be, but never were in the first place

We are the parents our children have warned us against.

ARLINGTON, WASHINGTON—If you can't go home again, a drive through the old neighborhood doesn't have to suck.

We are now celebrating the fortieth anniversary of the Summer of Love; a cataclysmic social watershed that changed the world as we knew it and set us on our current path. Or maybe not. Prior to that time shirts matched and conformity ruled. Afterwards, we got wild fashion, wilder music and free thought. And don't forget the drugs. Prior to 1967 we had no widespread use of pot, speed, acid, Ecstasy, or coke. Now, aren't we better off today?

While this year's event didn't qualify as a "package" show, there were some similarities to last year's version. Both had four bands with a smattering of original members playing the expected crowd pleasers with more spontaneity and enthusiasm than you would expect. While everyone has aged, there was a healthy supply of young musicians onstage filling out the sound. Accordingly, enhanced ear-monitor technology and a generally well-behaved audience improved the ragged, uneven concert sound of the old days.

The differences were also historically appropriate. Last year, the four bands (Herman's Hermits, one Monkee, two Turtles and the Grass Roots) played the controlled environment of a state fair in a well-oiled presentation that allocated precise set lengths, finished on time and emptied the crowd in an orderly fashion. Anyone out of their assigned place was gently guided back to where they once belonged, peacefully at that. This year's model was a somewhat less structured. The entertainers (It's a Beautiful Day, Quicksilver Messenger Service, Big Brother and the Holding Company and Jefferson Starship) were more casual than last year's models. They retained unpredictability and an endearing sloppiness. It was also free, with no reserved seats. Anyone wanting to be closer would just move in front of someone else, who would then cede the space gracefully. When was the last time that happened?

The recent events respectively resembled their past counterparts. If you attended a package show in 1966 you would see the hits presented in a fast-paced format that was all about controlled enjoyment. A concert in the park would have a more random element. Free admission would be part of this, along with some political rhetoric (although this was presented this year as an afterthought). You'd see lots of color, a healthy amount of improvisation and some herky-jerky movement that qualified as dancing.

At this summer's lovefest, each band featured at least two "original" members, although after forty years these distinctions blur. Janis Joplin, of course, is no longer with us and has been replaced by Kathi McDonald (who first recorded with Big Brother in the early 1970s). Grace Slick has aged ungracefully, and her part is taken by Diane Magnano, a thirtysomething beauty who sings well enough but provides the eye-candy role. Hippies always appreciated the presence of a hot babe within certain boundaries, and this got a lot of fans to board the Airplane in the first place. Magnano misses some of the notes, and her "Lather" is dreadful. But she clearly loves her job.

If Magnano is not expressly slick, we really don't miss Grace. Part of this is physical, we are not sure how convincing a rotund sixty-eight-year-old would be, admonishing us to "remember what the dormouse said." Other than that, Slick deserves banishment to permanent obscurity for her excruciatingly stupid "if you can remember it, you weren't there" characterization of the time.

Both substitute singers have impossible pumps to fill, but they each provide credible substitutes for the absent heroines. McDonald is a dynamo; what she lacks in style she makes up for with shout. She hits the right notes and is a blast to watch. In this way, she matches her predecessor. But both Joplin and Slick had unique vocal timbres, which McDonald and Magnano can't match.

The new Starship gets high marks for enthusiasm; its "Volunteers" is as passionate as when the issues it raises were actually in play. Paul Kantner, looking a bit puffy, has lost none of his commitment. David Freiberg, the other Starship charter member who did double duty with Quicksilver, sings well but looks like someone's befuddled Jewish uncle. You are torn between asking him about the old days, or if that was him at your Bar Mitzvah.

Looks are a superficial measure of anyone's worth, but many of us want to see how well these people have aged. Kantner and Freiberg, at least, aren't pretending to be anything they are not.

Many people today, if they remember 1967 at all, recall it through a hazy romanticism colored by everything that happened since. You can't talk about the Monterey Festival without mentioning Woodstock, and then Altamont. Fortunately there are movies of all three, so we can see the birth, rise and fall of the festival experience, at least through filmmakers' eyes. Pretty soon their recollections become ours, and even those who attended might not be sure where their own memory ended and the films began. I remember people who saw the Woodstock movie multiple times, and were convinced they were actually there.

Today, we can make our own movies. Indeed, an amateur can never match the power and spontaneity of Monterey or Woodstock. Most venues won't even allow you inside with a camera, so getting any kind of real footage is out of the question. But these people didn't care. I walked to the edge of the stage with a small video camera, shooting full performances head-on with no interference. If the sound leans too close to the bass side, it is nothing short of amazing what you can do with a camera and a computer these days. And to allow normal people (like myself, more or less) near enough to the stage democratizes the process.

A few weeks after this concert, the "real" event took place in its original epicenter, San Francisco's Golden Gate Park. It was an all-day affair, with some serious nostalgia. Marty Balin, who skipped the trip to the boonies, joined Starship onstage. Peripheral bands like Moby Grape and Canned Heat also appeared. Press reports were pretty gloomy, with musicians chastising the public for not living up to their promise and potential. There was war then, they told us, and there is still war today.

But this was one time I was glad to have been in the hinterlands. I attended 1987's 20th Anniversary in Golden Gate Park and found it to be pretty unwelcoming. The people who were there for the original event treated the "newcomers" with distaste.

If we are celebrating love, there should be no place for condescending recollections. And if this trend continues, the eventual anniversary will consist of a grumpy group on a huge park bench, whining about how everything was so much better back in the old days.

When that happens I'll just stay home, listening to *After Bathing at Baxters* on whatever playback format that is in use at the time. You can't ever forget that the music is what made this all worthwhile in the first place.

Talented

———

Sept. 11, 2011, Port Townsend, Washington

IN A PREVIOUS LIFE YOU went to several concerts a month, when those who are now rock-and-roll dinosaurs walked the earth. Today you live in a rural area and don't get out as much. But in August the music made a house call.

Garth Hudson ponders.

The month began with a spirited performance by Taj Mahal, who was headlining a local blues festival, and ended with something that promised to be extraordinary: a rare performance by Garth Hudson, the remarkable multi-instrumentalist who was one-fifth of The Band. He was touring with his wife Maud, about whom you knew nothing apart from the fact that she sings and is in a wheelchair.

You are working for the local paper as a news reporter, and interviewing Garth is one of your perks. This is eagerly anticipated but becomes one of the most difficult and challenging interviews you have ever done. He talks slowly (which makes transcription a lot easier) and provides detailed answers that border on college musicology lectures. Any attempt to talk about Bob Dylan, or fame, or anything concrete is rebuffed in favor of historical tales about how Bach walked two hundred miles to learn from one of his idols.

"This is amazing when you consider what they wore on their feet in those days," he says wryly. He later repeats the line onstage.

"This is great information and a lot of fun," you want to say. "But what I really need is a quote." You ask one question, he answers another. The interaction is more like a history lesson, since the facts are obscure and detailed and you have no real control over the conversation.

You talk to him through a Bluetooth system in your car and tape the conversation with a device on the passenger seat. When it is over you hang up and start the car and the radio blares out "Ophelia," The Band's last big single, and you interpret this as a good sign.

You would not think it to look at him, but Garth was famous long ago as the musical colorist for The Band, a group that rivaled The Beatles or anyone else for their songwriting, performance, and all-around aura. These days they are reduced on radio to a handful of famous tracks, but their potency cannot be overstated. They first performed "The Weight," now a modern hymn, and a partnership with Bob Dylan offered a peaceful musical refuge amid what could be (not always negatively) described as overwhelming artistic chaos.

The Band made it clear from the beginning that it was not like everybody else. The first notes of the first song of their first album, "Tears of Rage," sounded mournful and dissonant to the average pop fan. Many of us had to listen to the record several times before we were able to "get it."

Not at all like today, where kids listen to a few notes of one song before skipping to the next. The Band would never have survived such a lack of scrutiny.

There are other similarities between The Band and The Beatles. They both had an eight-year recording career and went out as the crowd called out for more. And they were a unit, where success resulted from an equally configured blend of voices and instruments. Taking one away was akin to removing a car wheel or a table leg.

Which is why many fans welcomed Garth to town, even though he was the functional equivalent of Ringo.

The first inkling that something could go awry comes with a late night call from Eric, the musician who is managing the tour. He is driving into town and wondering where they can go to eat at that hour and you remind him that all restaurants aside from McDonald's close by ten. You hear Maud in the background asking for "a steak to go that we can heat up later," which you are not inclined to supply because you have already loaned them money for a hotel.

You check them in. Later you are chatting with Eric in the parking lot when Garth comes out of the hotel and tells you that Maud is "dreadfully allergic" to mosquitoes and we should go to the front desk to get a vacuum cleaner, so we can suck the insects off of the ceiling. The front desk closed hours before Garth arrived, so that isn't an option. So you lend them your vacuum cleaner and hope you get it back in working order.

The next night Eric's band opens the show and plays until the Hudsons arrive. Eric introduces them and the audience hoots with pleasure and then watches respectfully as Garth wheels Maud into the club and down a ramp to the stage.

After a while the crowd's mood shifts from starstruck fascination to irritation and impatience. Garth putters around the stage setting up as if the audience doesn't exist. No one strikes up a conversation because the man is working, but he's not moving very quickly. Just when you are about to lose patience and go home they start playing, and you have to admit they sound pretty good. Eric's band is crisp, although Maud's vocals are all over the map. She kills on a version of "Don't Do It," and her reading of "The Weight" gives the standard its due.

You enjoy the experience. But several people stop you on the street telling you of their disappointment in the show, and with you for recommending it.

The music sounds great because it almost didn't happen. Eric sent a friend to pick up Garth and Maud but the guy got his signals crossed and used a key to enter the room. This caused the musicians to barricade themselves in their room for a while, finally agreeing to appear for the show after you arrive at the hotel along with Mark, the club owner.

Both of you sit patiently in the hall as the Hudsons prepare for the stage, where the audience is waiting. Mark, who has a lot to lose if it all goes south, isn't especially nervous. But you are. The next evening you are once again roped into picking them up at the hotel. This time you wait an hour before they finally emerge, and Maud is luminous. They have just worked out a new arrangement for "This Wheel's On Fire," a Band song they rarely perform. Once at the club it all starts over. Garth takes his time wheeling Maud in and starts tinkering again. You decide to cut your losses, go home, play with your cat, and catch up on your correspondence.

The idea came to you the day before, how you could use this proximity to Garth to write something exclusive and special. You decide to take him to an antique pipe organ that was reconstructed in a local church. If you could get Garth to the church, you would have an exclusive video, a rare taped performance and be able to write a compelling news story about a unique event.

It should be simple enough. You call Stan, the guy who rebuilt the organ, and explain that Mr. Hudson can't be rushed. Stan is accommodating, agreeing on our time range, while only requiring an hour's notice to get things started. Garth is a little harder to convince, but he seems to agree after he talks to Barney, who promises to bring along a tape recorder.

Mindful of Garth's slowness, you work backwards: The church building closes at six p.m. and Stan says we need an hour, so Garth needs to commit by around four thirty. At five thirty Eric calls and says Garth is ready. Right now you have more respect for Stan's time than Garth's, so you pull the plug, telling Eric "that ship has sunk."

It docks in another harbor. Eric takes Garth and Maud to an organ site two towns away and well out of your newspaper's circulation area, where they spent several hours making music and discussing history.

The event was unrecorded, aside from some pictures and a few moments of video Eric managed to snag for himself.

You are disappointed you were not there, and wonder if a great musician plays an antique organ in an empty house with three people listening and nothing ends up on YouTube, if that makes a sound anymore.

Soon enough the thrill is gone and you are more concerned about getting Garth and Maud out of the hotel in time than attempting to gather more material for any future story. While observing their slow departure, it's clear that Garth doesn't recognize anyone else's authority, so you can either play along or not. But if you play along you'll end up pitching in.

A few days later you run into a local musician who had worked the soundboard for Garth's second night, and witnessed the procrastination firsthand. He does not say what you would expect. He tells you that Garth is a true musical genius and follows his own path, which has nothing to do with what others expect of him.

Later you talk to Mark, whom you would also expect to have a bitter taste, but his strongest impression of Garth has to do with his devotion to Maud. "Whatever he does has to do with taking care of her," he said. Which explains the grand entrance of Garth pushing Maud up to the stage, as he is showing us his priorities. And his insistence on acquiring a vacuum cleaner at midnight to suck the mosquitoes off the ceiling evolves into a romantic act.

In a previous life you went to several concerts a month. One high point was in 1971, when Taj Mahal opened for The Band. That night Taj walked onstage alone in front of 10,000 people and played a casual set of acoustic blues. He was followed by a strong set from The Band, which was at the height of its powers.

Forty years on, Garth, at seventy-four, is the casual one. He is only five years older than Taj but the difference is startling. Taj is kinetic throughout: breezing into town in the early afternoon, meeting a group of students, playing a crisp, professional show at night and getting back on the bus. Garth is deliberate, taking one slow step at a time.

Commitments are only suggestions, whether they are to begin playing at the advertised start time, or leave the hotel by checkout. It happens when it happens, or it might not happen at all. We must accept this, since he brings the gift of music that arrives on its own terms.

The Band shone so brightly that a powerful magic stuck to everyone who was around, and Garth is still carrying around his share. There are some who don't see the glow, like the people who wanted to charge extra for the Hudsons being two and a half hours late getting out of their hotel room. Garth says they need to stay later and they don't want to pay any more money. Usually that works, because the one time we see Garth show any real emotion is when the routine fails to convince.

After a few weeks and a certain perspective sets in, you get it: Garth ignores the rules because he can. His talent must be a blessing and a burden; he comes to town and people cater to his whims, in return attempting to project their impression of what he should be.

So you feel a bit churlish as you recall Garth's last words to you as he left town: "I hope we meet again when everything will be perfect."

Testimony

Lately you've wondered if this whole music thing has gotten out of hand, whether it was a tremendous waste of time. You can't quantify the money you've spent on records, tapes, CDs, digital and records again. Or the magazines, books and concerts, along with the energy expended getting there. You could have used all this time to do something more useful, like writing books about things that matter or raising children who could change the world instead of trying to leave your own sorry mark.

"Authentic" used to be such a big word to you, it doesn't seem to mean anything to you now.

Eric Burdon doesn't much like the sun, Seattle 2013

In the beginning it was all about who was in the band when it started. So one without all of the significant original members, or even the bass player, wasn't ever good enough.

The changes were hard to take. The Hollies were inconceivable without Graham Nash. Alan Price fled The Animals in 1965; the next year Eric Burdon got rid of the old band and started running with a new litter.

Which made sense. People grow up together, then grow apart. Band members leave for various reasons. The most common reason is that one member is getting too much attention. Some leave because they don't play all that well, while others split up because they never really liked each other in the first place.

It was easier to accept the Hollies without Graham Nash than some other disasters. The Hermits without Herman, billing themselves as "Herman's Hermits," bounding onstage so enthusiastically that you weren't really sure Peter Noone wasn't there until halfway into the first song.

Here, you can still be surprised. In 1985 you saw the Beau Brummels, who did "Laugh Laugh" and "Just A Little," in a small bar in Marin County. It became a mutual admiration experience. The guitar player was impressed that you worked for *PC Magazine*, as you were for his participation in two of the 1960s' greatest songs.

At first, you felt cheated if an original or essential member wasn't in the band, after a while you found that it didn't always suck. You saw the original Animals during a 1983 reunion tour, thrilling enough, but the current pack is turbocharged by performances eclipsing the musicianship of the original guys. You feel disloyal admitting that the new-model Beach Boys with founding singer Mike Love as the only original member isn't completely terrible.

Not easily defined, your standards can exclude people on a whim for no good reason. Sounding good was the first test. The second level is earned when the substitute players are stupid, uncomfortable or verging on parodies of the originals.

Pretty soon it became unlikely, or impossible, to get all the original guys on the same stage. Or even the same room. You realize the new guys have a better sound than the originals, at least live. The ultimate decider is if the sound is any good or if it stirred up the right memories.

With a veteran band, there are lots of ways where it might go. The most rewarding is a group that is fronted by one of their essential members. Most of the backing musicians are new; sometimes the lead performer is twice their age. They are able to provide a mix of hits and versions of those not so well known. You've hit the jackpot if they play something new that's any good.

That doesn't happen a lot, if ever anymore. Graham Nash once told you that his new songs were every bit as good as the old chestnuts and there were still a few new tricks left in the old dog. That the new songs were "better" than the old ones missed the point, as their greatness had as much to do with what was happening to you at the time, and what was happening in the world, as the song itself.

You can't turn time back but you can go to a casino.
The difference between also ran casino-bound bands and performers like the Rolling Stones, Paul McCartney or The Who is production values, size and scope. Even people who don't want to leave the safety of the couch know that a large crowd is more exciting than a small one.

In either case when there is energy and commitment, it qualifies as a "win" even if the original records still sound better.

The best players, original or substitute, realize this and don't attempt to clone the old performances. They always add some new twist or turn that evokes a recollection while making you glad to be watching.

Some of these songs are fifty years old, during which time these performers' cellular makeup has changed several times over and they are now completely different people from those who made the original records. Who couldn't give an identical-as-the-old-days performance even if they wanted to.

A band with an original member backed by a crew of ringers earns points for enthusiasm, as long as they show a love for songs they've rehearsed hundreds of times before earning the chance to go onstage and play them thousands more.

Herman's Hermits can be a lot of fun. You have to laugh at how Peter Noone stretches "I'm Henry the Eighth, I Am" into the same approximate length as "In-a-Gadda-da-Vida."

Aside from Eric Burdon's outfit the best ringer band is the Beach Boys. Led by founding singer Mike Love and supported by his smarmy lieutenant Bruce Johnston, the group plays thirty songs in a breakneck ninety minutes. They are all familiar—too familiar—but for the most part, sound pretty good.

The Beach Boys live on because they perform in large halls to enthusiastic crowds. Performers feed off of audience energy, so that buoyancy pumps up the game. A smaller or less ambulatory audience gives off less energy, the musicians act accordingly.

The new-model Beach Boys and Animals play the same venues always performing familiar songs; you have never seen them when they did not perform "Surfin' USA" or "House of the Rising Sun," respectively. The difference is that Eric Burdon releases a new album every few years, drawing from them in concert, while the Beach Boys appropriate similar-themed songs from the same era that they didn't perform in the first place.

But nothing prepares you for The Association, playing in a half-filled high-school auditorium to a crowd of—there's no other way to say it—old people. There are two founding members, twice that as the Beach Boys, but that doesn't excuse performances of "Joy to the World" and "I Heard It Through the Grapevine," songs they had no business doing. At least the Beach Boys' appropriated covers are in the same area code as their regular stuff.

You duck out of The Association concert when they begin their horrendous medley and return for the show's final minutes. They play "Windy," "Cherish" and "Along Comes Mary," at wheelchair tempos.

The crowd applauds, worshipping an emperor that has no fucking clothes at all.

We all get old, but it's more apparent with people who were in the public eye when they were young. Once past sixty, they look nothing like rock stars. Later pictures of Freddie "and the Dreamers" Garrity showed an overweight, bald British guy. Throw a stick down a London street and you'd hit dozens of them. Jefferson Starship's David Freiberg now looks like a befuddled uncle who's wandered into the wrong Bar Mitzvah.

You are one click past sixty, and it is different than what you had imagined. You are now happier, more accomplished, more confident and better-looking than ever. You have improved with age.

So you feel for Garrity, Freiberg and many others whose finest hour occurred while in their twenties. The dream was over too soon for everyone.

Fans miss the original moments, where they were and what they are doing, but they have created different lives, while the surviving performers weren't sure what to do with themselves.

While you have evolved, these performers have stood still. To this day, some are playing the same old songs to diminishing audiences, trying to beam into the past when they were fab.

You retired as a rock journalist in late 2014 but was more than a year until you (or anybody else) noticed.

You began writing about music out of the belief your opinions were as good as anyone else in print, or even better. It started with record reviews and you scored three high-profile interviews before you got out of community college. This took some courage and provided a boost. Although the reviews were obsequious and the interviews were disjointed. You had not yet learned that an interview is close to a conversation, and is ruined when you are focused on the next question while your subject is in the middle of answering the last one.

With an assignment, you could get in close-up, write a review and sometimes even got paid. Clients appeared serially, including the *Globe and Mail*, *Rolling Stone Online*, web sites like *Mr. Showbiz* and *Sonic Boom*. As paid assignments trickled away you decided to write for free, if it got you into the door.

You've stopped writing but are not all-the-way cured. A few times a year something arrives that you want to see, and are tempted to come out of retirement. The urge passes. When you see a Facebook post about a magazine called RockCellar that is looking for writers, you are looking at the qualifications before remembering you don't do this anymore. You may write again, right now it's a better idea to just buy tickets to the show.

Not so long ago you needed to be down in front and up close. This meant you never saw Bruce Springsteen or the Rolling Stones. You would not pay money or take time out to fight crowds for nosebleed seats with no clear view or general admission standing-room-only situations.

Today, you are content to sit in the cheap seats. Soon enough the music gains a clarity missing since the early days. As if you'd been in the front row of the same movie for years before realizing the best seats were in the center of the theater.

They never liked you.
In journalism school you didn't have the same goals as your classmates. It was right after Watergate and they were out to change the world, topple crooked politicians and raise awareness about such issues as the environment and race inequality. You just wanted to meet rock stars and actresses.

You'd finished two years of college and needed to declare a major, and journalism was as good as anything. This occupation gave you a license to meet the people you admired in a more equal setting that hanging out after the show or walking up to them on the street.

Aside from meeting them you wanted them to like you. You attempted to astound them with your knowledge of and affection for their music, while asking unique questions they wouldn't get anywhere else.

That didn't seem to work very well, and you got better answers with an open-ended question that was a bit obvious. Some performers only wanted to answer what they'd rehearsed and others—David Crosby comes to mind—gave the answers that they wanted, regardless of the questions asked.

You were well into your fifties before realizing that none of the people you interviewed were ever going to like you. They forgot you existed as you left the room or hung up the phone, and they perceived any further contact as an intrusion.

You were part of their job. They would be courteous yet detached. Richard Thompson was the best example of this. You interviewed him several times and he would answer politely and in some detail. It was a performance, but it was always clear that he'd rather communicate through music. And he always appeared to be laughing at you, not with you.

When you met the Bee Gees in 1975 they were so nice you believed they actually liked you. Later on you saw this trick used by musicians, politicians and activists, looking at you with such intensity and focus you became the most important thing in the world. The truth was when you left the room the next "most important thing" would sit in the same chair and you were forgotten.

You met Barry and Maurice Gibb in their hotel room and it went really well. Or so you thought. They told you the plans for their new movie, to be called *The Bull on the Barroom Floor.*

"It's somewhat of a Western," Barry told you. "It's about three English boys who emigrate to America in the early days and bring a bull with them and mate it. It's very fast. It's supposed to be a chase film, which hasn't been done in years."

You mentioned the movie in the story, an exclusive. A few months later you discovered that it was a lie. Upon arriving in Boston you learned that one of your classmates had interviewed them a few days before you, and told you how the Bee Gees made the whole thing up on the spot. They were sitting in a bar, and a drunken Maurice Gibb said he would mention the project in his next interview. Which turned out to be you.

Years later you were in a Chicago bookstore when you opened a massive Bee Gees biography and scanned the index to find a reference to the fake film. Those scoundrels had spun the same tale to many unsuspecting reporters, who at the time believed that the Bee Gees actually liked them.

It wasn't all negative. Once you decided they weren't ever going to like you the goal became to have a worthwhile conversation where you might be able to learn something, either about the artist or about life.

Even that became less interesting in a world where any yahoo could become a blogger and request an interview. This cut your choices since someone really famous won't talk to a blogger but your lot—writing for several random music websites—wasn't much better.

The final step in your recovery was realizing there are no unique questions. Your interview victim has heard and answered them all before, and there is no good reason for you to be there. You end up in a room or on the phone with a famous person acting out a play that is of interest to no one, even the participants.

Your music collection has returned to where it began.

You've had some version of a collection from the time you acquired your first 45, and have purchased the same music several times over; changing formats every few years before ending up right where you started.

You began with 45s, moving up to mono albums and then stereo. You skipped four-track and eight-track tapes, dabbling briefly with reel-to-reel before beginning a prolonged involvement with cassettes. When you moved to New Mexico, you left the LPs at your parents' house and carried around the cassette collection, whose sound soon warped as the tapes deteriorated.

Returning East, you took back your five hundred-or-so LPs but began selling them off and trading them for CDs four years later. CDs were the best format so far; you weren't worried about scratches and skips and could play the whole of *Tommy* or *Electric Ladyland* without needing to get off the couch.

You found yourself purchasing the same album on CD that you'd already bought on vinyl and cassette. The early CD releases were flawed; later there would soon be a better-sounding edition with bonus tracks. You scarfed those up before realizing there was a reason that the "bonus" tracks weren't on the original album. Many of them were flat-out terrible, or they ruined the record's continuity.

After collecting several hundred CDs, original albums and enhanced repackages, you climb aboard the digital train because you can theoretically carry a music collection in your pocket and listen to it anywhere. You can add CDs to the digital data bank but end up creating a new collection of downloaded songs because they are so inexpensive, but you lose track of these purchases because there is no tangible connection to the music. So you are surprised when you go online to buy a vinyl edition of Neil Young's *Tonight's the Night*, to then discover you already owned the album in digital form.

Around ten years ago you began collecting album covers as art, popping them into square frames and hanging them up around the house. The criteria: they are great albums with great covers released between 1965 and 1975, more or less. You gather about thirty of them before it begins to annoy your visitors and the collection has run its course.

You acquire a turntable with the purpose of digitizing albums but soon find the vinyl experience engaging, a better way to connect, actually re-connect, with the music. Vinyl records are self-contained, with good and not-so-good music on each one. You can't skip ahead. You need to make a new decision every twenty or thirty minutes. Soon enough you are close to five hundred again, having inherited your mother's collection when she sold her house and moved away. You reclaim the first LP you ever owned, The Beatles' *Second Album*, which still plays well enough.

You end up replacing many of the albums you once owned and some you missed the first time around. It is all about rediscovery, since you are getting new if not fresh versions of music you have purchased many times before.

First as a mono album, then in stereo. Cassettes, CDs, MP3s and back to mono albums, the starting point. Except time the albums are twice the thickness as the originals and, at around $25, about six times the price. It wasn't so long since this positions were reversed, with CDs costing twice as much as an equivalent LP.

For years you have bought music listening to it once, twice or not at all. One day, you said, life will slow down enough in order to enjoy all you have accumulated. That time should be now, but you end up staring at your collection with no idea what to play. So you give up, reading a book or taking a nap.

This getting older ain't for cowards.

In your generation, the best music was made by people in their 20s for those in their teens. Today, everyone then involved is in spitting distance of 70. Many of those who made the music are stuck in the past, still connecting to and attempting to relive the glory of their early days.

In 2000 you interviewed three members of Buffalo Springfield, those who were not Neil Young and Stephen Stills. You spent an evening with drummer Dewey Martin, who was hours late because he couldn't find his other shoe. He spent much of the time criticizing Stills and Young, who would not allow him to tour under the "Buffalo Springfield" moniker. You held your tongue because you agreed with Stills and Young, declining Martin's invitation for an early morning breakfast. At the end of the assignment you had the most respect for guitarist Richie Furay, who had become a minister when his music career wound down.

Death has always hovered in the background. While you were in high school you lost several players to misadventure, at the height of their powers. The death of Jimi Hendrix in 1970 was a shock, since you had seen him play a year before and were certain that he would grow older and greater. He had so much potential, you mused, not connecting it to how your parents and teachers were saying the same thing about you.

The Hendrix legend grew through myriad record releases and the efforts by the survivors to reconstruct what he would have done if he had lived. This incomplete feeling was because he'd left at the top. The Beatles broke up the same year, leading fans to scour the past for undiscovered gems and incessantly hope the band would get back together again—even after John Lennon's death.

Both Hendrix and the Beatles built an astonishing body of work in a short time. Still, you were looking for more. You dreamed about a new Beatles album so frequently that its existence spilled into your waking life. That you should be satisfied with what existed never entered your mind.

Later on, the musicians showed their mortality by dying from what could be described as natural causes. This underscored another shift: "David Bowie, he died too young," you heard when the 69-year-old died in 2016. This from the same group who once parroted the "don't trust anyone over 30" homily. Like everything else, your generation changed the rules about aging as it happened to them.

And aging happens to you. You realized a while ago that you can no longer complete the daily routines that were once effortless. You finally have the opportunity to join a softball team before determining that you couldn't make a convincing run around the bases. There is the technology, which has allowed placing entire music libraries on a one-inch-square device, to be enjoyed during long walks or bike trips. This can keep you moving. Or you can sit in a chair; watching and listening to the media collection you have accumulated through the years. Add the Internet to create an interactive cultural experience.

You haven't yet experienced the inevitable dementia or debilitating disease, which could confine you to a physical space while allowing your mind to run free. For these times you imagine an immersive setup with virtual glasses and headphones that are controlled by wiggling your nose.

Isolating, for sure. But there are worse ways to grow old.

It doesn't belong to you anymore.

There were a lot of rules, in the beginning. The best bands were always bright, original and didn't repeat themselves from one song to the next. The original artists were sacred, and cover versions were never as good. The Hollies' "If I Needed Someone" was weak next to the brilliant Beatles take. Even in a department store, you could tell if the song over the speaker was from the original Beatles or a shoddy imitator. If it wasn't the real thing it wasn't any good.

A lot of rules. And you were only eleven.

Things changed, beginning with Joe Cocker's breathtaking "A Little Help From My Friends" cover in 1968. It was then clear that Beatles songs could benefit from other views. You eventually became more accepting, admitting that cover versions of Beatles songs didn't have to suck. You watched a group of high-school kids perform the entire *Revolver* in 2006, and another group play all of *Sgt. Pepper* seven years later. The performances were necessarily ragged. Once you would have run away screaming in pain for the sacrilege, but these days the beauty of the songs and the dedication to the music yields happiness and light. You are buoyed by the idea of these songs being taught in music class, morphing into next generation folk songs.

These generations will recognize the Beatles and Bob Dylan as similar to Beethoven and Shakespeare. You are privileged to have witnessed the creation of this art, but it no longer belongs to you and your ilk. Reminding people who are new to this music how you were there at the beginning can appear churlish and condescending. It should be enough to observe the joy of discovery, as people find meaning in the music outside of its historical context.

You no longer resent the repetition of the same stories, even if they get the details wrong. You tolerate the various anniversary editions of major records but rarely purchase an upgrade. News of a re-release usually drives you toward repeated listenings of the versions in your library.

It no longer matters whether you were "there" or not, because it doesn't belong to you anymore. Perhaps it never did. There is no one alive today who knew Beethoven or Shakespeare. Soon enough, your own recollections will be in the wind.

Unless you write some of them down.

Life's been good to you, so far.

If this is the time for listening to, watching and reading all of the music, movies and books you have accumulated in no particular order, random thoughts accompany the process. Some are profound, others are profane. Some you forget seconds later; others you remember long enough to capture them.

You have lived through a historical time, with political, cultural and technological changes, but are somewhat uncertain about how the world is shaping up. You won't complain about kids these days, their music and that it was oh so much better "back in the day." Whenever that was. Truth is, the unbroken connection to the world's minutiae can only be a good thing. The biggest change is that you once went after knowledge as if it were water: visiting bookstores, libraries and places to learn and observe.

When you tell people you went to Woodstock, or saw Bob Dylan, or interviewed George Harrison, they act awestruck and respectful. At the time it was just another thing that made your life really cool. Now it doesn't seem real, to others and yourself. There may be some that is lost in the mists of time, but none of your recollections are flat-out wrong. That you know of.

You remember dismissing old people when you were young, and are grateful that people half your age acknowledge your existence and recognize your accomplishments. Which are really nothing special. You were simply born at the right time, which put you in the right place.

Once you are able to filter in the most important information, technology is a good thing. You often take long walks in the woods and on the beach listening to music on a device that holds every song that you really liked. At these times you realize how the music has changed your life and times, and there was never a necessity to search for deeper meaning, to dissect the musicians' lives or to meet the artists.

Not so long ago you needed to know everything and sit in the epicenter, to be right where everything was taking place. Today it is enough to sit still and listen to the music while it evokes the past and shapes the future.

Transcript/2

———

FILE AS: radio script 9/27/16

Cue "When I'm Sixty-Four" beginning in background

Paul McCartney wrote this wistful view of aging at sixteen years old, while the teenaged Pete Townsend had a different view off the golden years yet to come.

"Things they do look awful cold/hope I die before I get old."

The song "My Generation" could only have been written by someone very young in a blast of chaotic energy, looking toward an uncertain future. At the time it was impossible for Townshend or anyone else—to make a believable prediction. So he and others grabbed the first phrase that came into their heads to describe what they were feeling at the time.

Back in the 1960s, many performers sought to move beyond silly love songs into other topics, so getting older—which everyone does—was the obvious choice. They used poetic license as a time machine, imagining their lives after they inevitably aged.

One of the most profound peeks through the prediction porthole came from Simon and Garfunkel, with their 1968 album *Bookends*. The killer track is

"Old Friends." Here, the twenty-seven-year-old Paul Simon contemplates aging from a young man's point of view, painting a picture that we can all see in our heads.

"A newspaper blown through the grass falls on the round toes of the high shoes of the old friends."

Simon lost some of his lyrical magic along the way with "Old" in 2000. He had lived half a lifetime, but his fifties were filled with a whole lot less poetry than his twenties.

"Now many wars have come and gone. Genocide still goes on. Buddy Holly still goes on But his catalog was sold. God is old. We're not old. God is old. He made the mold."

In 1972 Neil Young, then twenty-six, gave us "Old Man," written to the caretaker he inherited along with his new ranch. Here, he compares the goals and needs of the old and the young, concluding they are pretty much the same.

"Old Man take a look at my life, I'm a lot like you. I need someone to love the whole day through."

Kinks songwriter Ray Day-viss follows a different process in the recording of "Where Did My Spring Go." In this obscure little ditty Day-viss, at twenty-four, projects himself into the future and singing as an old man looking back. Pining for his youth and blaming his physical and psychological demise on a long ago girlfriend. It's scary and bitter, which is how Day-viss may have imagined himself at the time.

"When you were loving me you were just using me. You would employ me, you would destroy me. Now all I've got are varicose veins."

Most vintage artists release new music infrequently, a wise choice. They aren't drowning us in a series of observations about a sixty-year-old's angst. Their new songs, however wonderful, cannot possibly match the energy in what they created when their world was young.

Listening to old music from people who are still playing and singing is a little like scanning an old photo album. They were cute but often clueless. But it's still cool to know what they were thinking, even if it turned out to be nothing like we imagined.

Cue "When I'm Sixty-Four" ending.

This is Charlie Bermant for KWTK-FM; authentic, eclectic community radio in the valley and on the peninsula.

Charlie Bermant lives in the Pacific Northwest with his wife, Laura Bell, where he continues to find meaning in the music created during his lifetime. He is the author of *A Serious Hobby*, a collection of interviews, and *Imagine There's No Beatles*, a short work of investigative speculative fiction. You can find him at charliebermant@gmail.com.

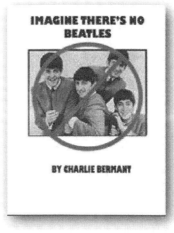

Made in the USA
Columbia, SC
07 August 2017